The Truth About
Thriving in Change

HR Leaders

"A must read for managers, Bill uses language with care, economy, and precision. Managing change is basically about helping people deal with uncertainty. This writing effectively uses a combination of practical experience, common sense, and humor in describing strategies designed to achieve desired results while maintaining morale and enhancing engagement."

Michael Mimnaugh, Vice President, Human Resources,
Sony Corporation of America

"Challenging long-accepted common sense, the 'Truths' will cause all of us involved with managing change to look in the mirror—and certainly to get away from our desks."

Patricia Kelly Schmitt, Vice President, Human Resources,
Global Animal Health and Consumer HealthCare,
Schering-Plough Corporation

"This book is truly a practical resource for leaders on how to handle the multitude of personal and professional challenges faced by managers every day. The content is well organized in a logical, easy-to-use format with each truth presented in a bite-sized, easily digested segment. I would recommend this book to managers searching for 'Truths' on how to enhance their effectiveness in constantly changing business environments."

Thomas G. Moran, Vice President, Human Resources,
Thomson Publishing

"To be inspiring, to be tough and empathic, to set a vision, and to move an organization toward audacious goals is frightening and often overwhelming. This page-turner takes the essentials and breaks the process into 49 Truths—easy to adopt behaviors and watch-outs—that are easy to read, remember, and bring to life daily."

Dede LaMarche, US HR Business Partner,
FMC Agricultural Products Group

Academia

"This book is about a set of propositions that you, as a leader, can call on for all occasions dealing with the management of change. Bill has organized the collective wisdom, stated in the form of 'Truths', which can guide novices, seasoned corporate veterans, and those of us in the midst of organization transitions. You will be able to compare your ideas with concise and precisely stated maxims that will stimulate you to become even more articulate about developing your own versions of the 'Truths' about change. That is worth the price of admission!"

Charles Seashore, Ph.D., Professor, Fielding Graduate University

"Many students are under the impression that a graduate degree will impart all wisdom, but what they fail to recognize is that there is no substitute for experience. What Bill's book does so well is to impart his substantial experience—along with the textbook knowledge—to move you ahead in your career. If you manage people or projects, the wisdom found within each 'Truth' will help keep you on the leading edge of your profession. This is a reference guide that belongs in your library."

Stuart J. Lipper, Senior Director of MBA Programs,
Rutgers Business School,
Rutgers, The State University of New Jersey

Business/Human Resources Consultants

"This is a worthwhile read for any and all managers. It flows topically and builds in an integrated fashion. The format is reader-friendly and the messages are 'tried and true,' while avoiding the usual boilerplate platitudes. You cannot help but come away with some ideas on how to improve your change management skills."

Robert M. Marino, President, Alpha Nouveau Consulting, Inc.

"With business acumen, a human resources perspective, and behavioral research as the writing's fundamental underpinnings, this book quenches the long and desperate thirst of managers in the corporate community on how to lead a team through the sometimes-dizzying maze of change."

William D. Cassidy III, Ph.D., President,
Human Resources International LLC

"Anyone interested in changing people and changing organizations will want this book in their library. It provides important insights into organizations and their need for change, yet recognizes that authentic change comes from within people. Only by changing people can we change organizations. Bill provides valuable discussion of the information, decision criteria, and tools needed to accelerate the change process. Its power lies in its simplicity, accessibility, and pragmatism."

Richard W. Beatty, Ph.D., Coauthor of *The Workforce Scorecard*

"Rooted in research and personal experience, Bill's writing is true to its purpose—offering a therapeutic blend of wisdom, compassion, and highly practical application that will undoubtedly help leaders overcome what ails them and their organizations, and allow them not just to survive but to *thrive* in continuous change."

Laurie Murphy, President, PeopleAreKey, Inc.

Training and Development Practitioners

"Years of designing and delivering training programs have taught me that managers value short, practical guides to various subjects. They will not be disappointed here. The 'Truths'—and their practicality—are an ideal basis for personal effectiveness enhancement or leadership development."

David J. Owen, Vice President, Global Learning & Development, International Flavors & Fragrances, Inc.

"Although we know that change is constant, we are always surprised by it. Bill provides a roadmap to successfully navigate corporate change. Being conscientious to follow the 'Truths' will enable people to successfully face any organizational challenge."

Rosina Racioppi, President and Chief Operating Officer, WOMEN Unlimited, Inc.

Operations/Manufacturing/General Management

"Having been involved over my 33 year career with 7 different companies that were experiencing significant change, 5 of which I was CEO, I related to the 'Truths.' I especially enjoyed the brevity and clarity in which the points were made. It functions more like a guide, providing straightforward examples that drive the point and makes for easy reading and future referral."

Brian Fitzpatrick, President and Chief Executive Officer,
Bentley Labs LLC

"Bill clearly demonstrates that successful change doesn't come in a can; he provides practical tools and sound advice that can be applied to achieve the desired results of any change effort."

Mike Ruiz, Director of Process Integration, North Jersey Media Group

THE TRUTH ABOUT
ABOUT

THRIVING IN CHANGE

William S. Kane

© 2008 by Pearson Education, Inc.
Publishing as FT Press
Upper Saddle River, New Jersey 07458

FT Press offers excellent discounts on this book when ordered in quantity for bulk purchases or special sales. For more information, please contact U.S. Corporate and Government Sales, 1-800-382-3419, corpsales@pearsontechgroup.com. For sales outside the U.S., please contact International Sales at international@pearsoned.com.

Company and product names mentioned herein are the trademarks or registered trademarks of their respective owners.

Printed in the United States of America

First Printing May 2008

ISBN-10:   0-13-235462-4
ISBN-13: 978-0-13-235462-2

Pearson Education LTD.
Pearson Education Australia PTY, Limited.
Pearson Education Singapore, Pte. Ltd.
Pearson Education North Asia, Ltd.
Pearson Education Canada, Ltd.
Pearson Educatión de Mexico, S.A. de C.V.
Pearson Education—Japan
Pearson Education Malaysia, Pte. Ltd.

Library of Congress Cataloging-in-Publication Data

Kane, William S.
  The truth about thriving in change / William S. Kane.
      p. cm.
  Includes bibliographical references.
  ISBN 0-13-235462-4 (pbk. : alk. paper) 1. Organizational change. I. Title.
  HD58.8.K356 2008
  658.4'06--dc22

                          2007029607

Vice President, Publisher
Tim Moore

Associate Publisher and Director of Marketing
Amy Neidlinger

Acquisitions Editor
Jennifer Simon

Editorial Assistant
Pamela Boland

Development Editor
Russ Hall

Digital Marketing Manager
Julie Phifer

Marketing Coordinator
Megan Colvin

Cover and Interior Designs
Stuart Jackman,
Dorling Kindersley

Managing Editor
Gina Kanouse

Senior Project Editor
Lori Lyons

Copy Editor
Karen Gill

Design Manager
Sandra Schroeder

Senior Compositor
Gloria Schurick

Proofreader
San Dee Phillips

Manufacturing Buyer
Dan Uhrig

As a human resources practitioner, I have been fortunate in my 25-year career to be a student, participant, and leader of successful organizational change. And while the environments and industries have been diverse, my observations about these processes have yielded a common theme. For organizational change to have the highest probability for success, on any scale, management must clearly identify and align the vision, strategy, tactics, and collective values of the organization—as the catalysts and cornerstones of the desired end state.

Done properly, management can help organizational participants embrace change processes for the enterprise to be merged, stabilized, started up, or repositioned in a way to satisfy most stakeholders in a relatively condensed timeframe.

Less than optimal direction setting or poor execution leads to an erosion of employee motivation, engagement, and productivity. Commitment falls by the side, goal attainment becomes elusive, and everyone is running for the lifeboats.

This writing offers guidance and hope for managers trying to keep their head above water in times of rising tides by dispelling organizational myths and providing practical advice for the newly appointed supervisor, as well as the seasoned corporate veteran. It includes a combination of "tried-and-true" success stories, lessons learned from failures, "how-to" human resources advice, related anecdotes, and research from contemporary thought leaders about large and small-scale organizational change.

The ideas presented in this book aren't mutually exclusive, but they're universally applicable. Stylistically, some Truths are more conceptual, while others—with more comprehensive "to-do's"— should satisfy the most demanding pragmatists.

As a framework, I recognize that my professional experiences will not mirror yours, because every individual and organization is unique. However, I am confident that this writing can help you avoid a few bumps and foster your own individual capabilities for managing optimal and sustained performance.

Enjoy!

What is organizational change?

Coaching third-grade soccer is hard. It requires skills assessment, planning, discipline, and coordination. It involves blending talents and teaching the players to fight their natural tendency to chase the ball all at once. Plays must be carefully scripted and yet have allowances for some individual improvisation.

As the coach, it requires personal investment, energy, and patience. It causes you to keep fingers crossed with hope and an aspirin bottle nearby for frustration. However, there is no more enjoyable reward than watching the ball sail into the back of your opponent's net.

Organizational change shares all these characteristics, with some additional complexities. It's an ongoing journey with multiple destinations and no real endpoint. It's characterized by multiple contradictions—the need to balance a short- and long-term perspective; the need to blend or select conservative and liberal points of view; the ability to be objective when analyzing subjective matters; the talent to have patience when time is of the essence; and the ability to let go of old practices, processes, and mindsets while gravitating toward new ones.

For the purposes of this writing, managing change is the all-encompassing process by which you confront or overcome challenges or seize new opportunities by perpetually transforming the organization from its current state to a state deemed more desirable through tapping new or improved ideas, suggestions, and processes, and applying them toward previously unrealized potential.

The mantra of organizational change is "better, faster, and cheaper." Its three most important elements are speed, speed, and more speed.

The benefits of organizational change

Change, even for the sake of change, can have many benefits beyond process improvements, market share enhancement, or greater profitability. It offers individual and collective learning opportunities. It may also heighten employee engagement and interest in work, thus increasing productivity and job satisfaction. Likewise, employees will have a greater sense of pride and ownership if they participate.

What's different today?

Every generation has its business and economic challenges. The dialogue in today's corporate boardrooms and its ripple effect to the shop floors about the need for change is dramatically different and far more complex than it was even ten years ago.

First and foremost, bottom-line performance continues to be a mandate.

Second, the means to attain positive results is critical as stakeholders are demanding that ethics and organizational values be communicated and adhered to within an organization—at all levels and at all times. This includes having appropriate checks and balances (Sarbanes-Oxley, etc.) established for all aspects of corporate governance and policy.

Third, organizational leaders must be students of current events as the breadth and depth of issues to be considered, planned for, and reacted to expand on a global basis in real-time. Concerns about international political and economic instability have broad business implications.

Fourth, within domestic borders, organizational leaders must grapple with uncertainty in stock market valuations; quarter-to-quarter performance pressures; political, societal, and demographic shifts; technology changes; and inflationary concerns.

These changes—and others across the world and in our backyard—are happening faster and harder than ever, making related organizational change the primary and continuous challenge for all management. It takes real focus and fortitude to survive, much less prosper.

Is the time right?

Is the time *ever* right? In *The 7 Habits of Highly Effective People,* Stephen Covey speaks of a trap that often proves too attractive for many to resist. It seems a lumberjack had been working feverishly to cut down a large tree; however, he made only limited progress in several hours. When asked by a passerby why he did not take the time to sharpen the blade—to speed along his endeavor—the lumberjack replied that he was too busy sawing. Managing organizational change is a continual sharpening of the saw.

Is there a checklist you can follow?

Leading and managing change is about

- Your commitment
- Identifying the cause of and the need for change by analyzing your organization's strengths, weaknesses, opportunities, and threats (SWOT)
- Providing inspirational answers to "Why are we here?" "Where are we going?" "What needs to be accomplished?" and "How will we accomplish these objectives?"
- Creating your cultural and operating framework with the identification and inculcation of organizational values and desirable behaviors
- Treating everyone with respect and dignity
- Aligning people with purpose by getting the right person in the right place at the right time
- Managing performance
- Tracking progress
- Making every day better than the last

...and doing all of these things with proactive communication while wearing the hat of parent, teacher, field general, minister, confidante, coach, friend, referee, psychologist, and principal.

Is it fun?

Like a roller-coaster ride, the answer to this question largely depends on individual perspective. On the one hand, it's an exciting and invigorating process to lead, participate in, or have a fingerprint upon a process that raises the organization's collective ability to be more effective and efficient, and therefore, more competitive and viable. However, like many objectives worth working toward, such rewards can be attained only through what is likely to be a challenging and sometimes painful and difficult journey.

TRUTH

1

Life is 10% of what
happens to you and
90% of how you react

As managers, we work longer, smarter, and harder, but it seems that we can never get ahead. The pace of business is ever-increasing; expectations for results are in real-time; we're asked to make dozens of decisions per day, often with limited information; much work follows us home at the end of the already-far-too-long day; our span of control is stretched beyond capacity; and it seems that any energy and stamina are eroded by noon.

It isn't pretty, but it's reality. Change is a given. The chaotic "better, faster, and cheaper" world is here to stay.

In many respects, we don't have control over many of these dynamic business challenges; however, we can control how we react. The best indicator for us to personally monitor in this regard is stress.

Stress is somewhat difficult to define. It's a natural by-product of life—a subjective sensation associated with a variety of symptoms that differ for each of us. It involves mental, emotional, or physical tension, strain, or pressure. It touches all aspects of our lives, but it's particularly evident at work, where surveys and studies have shown that occupational fears and pressures are by far the leading source of stress in American workers' lives. And that trend is increasing.

Research says—contrary to popular opinion—that a certain amount of stress can be healthy, having a positive impact upon your productivity. Your heart rate, blood pressure, respiration, and metabolism all increase, helping your body react quickly and effectively to increased pressure or anxiety. By consequence, it helps you perform at a heightened level.

Stress gets a bad name when it takes over. Too much stress, such as derived from dealing with potential job insecurity or change, can be crippling. Emotional responses range from a sense of loss, much like grief, to eventual energy rejuvenation. Its early troubling stages include numbness, paralysis, irritability, and resistance.

> Research says—contrary to popular opinion—that a certain amount of stress can be healthy, having a positive impact upon your productivity.

Behavioral responses include one of four adaptation strategies: ignoring what is going on around us, clinging to existing myths and paradigms (fight); escaping through rationalization or a radical change in direction (flight); making some minor modification in our behavior (hoping that the situation will somehow change); or embracing the change as a new learning and application opportunity.

While it isn't your place to judge how others are reacting to and absorbing the transformation around them, it's important to be aware of the potential emotional and behavioral responses for self-monitoring, as well as to help others through the experience. To this end, there are some scientifically proven tips to deal with anger, frustration, and exhaustion—helping you keep your head while those about you are losing theirs.

First, recognize there may be some early ambiguity, misinformation, and confusion about possible courses of action for your business and your role during times of organizational change. Try to get the facts. There is some validity to concerning yourself only with the facts and not the company grapevine.

Second, hone your skills of awareness to recognize those times when you lose touch—with yourself and those you manage. Be conscious of your whole self, others, and the context in which you live and work.

Third, never lose your optimism. Hope is a guiding force. It contributes to recuperation and renewal. It enables you to believe in and strive to attain your goals for tomorrow. It lets you inspire others.

Fourth, have compassion by directing your attention to others. This is critical for your sustenance and maintenance of a leadership role.

Last, don't underestimate the power of rest and relaxation. Your parasympathetic nervous system, which counteracts stress, positively responds to recovery activities such as meditating, exercising, listening to music, reading, and enjoying other hobbies.

> Hope is a guiding force...It enables you to believe in and strive to attain your goals for tomorrow.

The next few Truths are intended to help you identify the important professional and personal factors to consider as you determine whether to participate in and manage the organizational change mandate.

TRUTH

2

If your values don't agree, it's probably time to flee

In her book *Is It Too Late to Run Away and Join the Circus?* Marti Smye suggests that matching your belief system with your employer's is more important than matching your skill set.

This harmonization is absolutely critical. More so when organizations are going through significant change—particularly in the early stages of the transformation, the collective and representative values of the organization are in a glaring spotlight. They're primarily evidenced by the way people behave, the way they're treated, and the decisions that are made.

> Matching your belief system with your employer's is more important than matching your skill set.

There once was a corporate leader so consumed with his desire to cut costs and to hastily make change that he ultimately lost his way. To the outside world, this gentleman had a most impressive educational and business pedigree, as well as a prior record of accomplishment. He traveled the globe, ate at the finest restaurants, went to the "right" shows and events, and carried a corporate title and compensation package worthy of it all. However, he was hardly out of central casting. Insiders were well aware of his Machiavellian approach and attitude. His caustic tyrants were rampant, and his volcano-like temper flared more than it settled. He had little patience, and he expected nothing short of "24/7" dedication from his team, treating them as if they were interchangeable parts. He ruthlessly closed plants, dramatically reduced the workforce, and sold off the businesses he deemed to be lacking—all in a manner of principle and practice that was contrary with the company's stated values. His actions quickly helped the balance sheet, but they inevitably threatened the actual viability of the business. His relentless pursuit of bottom-line performance had caused him to not respect or trust others.

When confronted with this type of situation, we have a range of choices—from ignorance to exodus. Each option has a significant personal and professional consequence. Your values will likely determine the path you take.

Values are a principle or an ideal that is intrinsically desirable. They help us shape and interpret the state of our world and aid in our understanding of how it works. They're derived from our upbringing and experiences—formed and influenced by our family, our friends, and those with whom we have significant relationships. They influence how we feel, think, react, and behave. They're based on social, religious, cultural and ethical grounding, and they're individually derived and experienced through occasions when we deal with the endpoints of the range of human emotions such as conflict, grief, disappointment, envy, and success.

All organizations, whether we're talking about IBM, the local parent-teacher organization, or the Girl Scouts, have explicit or implicit values as their cultural underpinning. The shared meanings and interpretations of these values help us understand the expectations for professional behavior, as well as gain a clear understanding about how to handle any potential conflicting demands.

The question and potential challenge for each of us is to identify and understand our personal values and determine if there is alignment with the way they're "lived" within our respective organization. This is where a little soul searching comes in handy.

We can't be "successful" by any definition in our organizational lives without broader harmony. Said differently, do you really want to work for an organization where you don't believe in the products or services, business model, culture, or decisions made by leadership of the enterprise? Do you want to work for someone who seems to have too cozy a relationship with various vendors? Do you want to work next to someone who is apathetic about the organization?

> The question and potential challenge for each of us is to identify and understand our personal values and determine if there is alignment with the way they're "lived" within our respective organization.

In search of values congruence, take time to reflect and compare. Know that whatever path you choose—whether you grin and bear it, take on the cause, or opt out—you'll hopefully come to find, as others have, that individuals with aligned values at home and at work generally experience higher consciousness, increased performance, heightened security, greater confidence, higher job satisfaction, higher morale, and more effective decision making.

TRUTH

3

Service awards aren't what they used to be

You have been with the company for several years, having made some friends along the way. You have learned some new tricks and stayed current with both functional and technological trends. Your performance reviews have always been good, and in many cases, exceeded expectations. You enjoy most of your coworkers, and you genuinely like your boss. Your work is gratifying, and you take pride in your contributions.

But somewhere in the back of your mind, despite the favorable job conditions and relationships, with change in the wind, you're a bit unsettled. You're beginning to feel the itch to move on.

Should you scratch?

It may give you some comfort (or raise your eyebrow) to know that you aren't alone in your thinking. One recent survey indicated that 66 percent of us would consider new job opportunities, while the most recent statistics from the Bureau of Labor Statistics showed that 20 percent of us saw fit to actually change jobs.

When you weigh your employment options, your time horizon is most relevant.

> One recent survey indicated that 66 percent of us would consider new job opportunities.

Short-term considerations

You should consider leaving if

- Your current role doesn't meet your professional needs or expectations, there is values dissonance, or you're "stuck" in a stage of your job with no signs of progression or rejuvenation on the horizon.

- You aren't having fun anymore. Your energy has faded, and there's no gas in the tank. You don't have the fortitude or appetite for playing some needed politics. The stress level is too high.

- You don't believe in the future of the organization. Repeated efforts to bring positive change have failed, and your hopes are diminished. Your frustration is inhibiting your view.

- You don't want to be in a position where your decisions will impact the careers and potential livelihoods of others.

■ Your relationship with your boss or coworkers is unhealthy and beyond repair.

While easier said than done for most of us, your options include looking for a new job, starting a new career, working for someone else, working for yourself, going back to school, doing temporary or contract work, or picking up roots.

You should consider staying if

■ You welcome the thought of being consulted on matters of strategy and business planning before the decisions are made. You'll have a real impact upon the future of the organization.

■ You have the chance to make the change agenda your agenda by developing new skills and expertise.

■ You'll learn about a new way of business thinking or perhaps help create the organization's new culture.

■ Your personal future looks secure and bright. You see the possibility for enhanced contribution or a promotional opportunity down the road.

■ You trust the senior management team, and they have a track record of success.

■ You are capable of leaving any and all selfish interests behind, embracing a genuine approach of servitude.

If these latter reasons (or others) resonate, put your seatbelt on!

Long-term considerations

While recent trends such as extended life expectancy, eroding retirement benefits, expanded training and educational opportunities, and other social and economic factors may keep you working longer than what you expected on the day of your high school graduation, your professional life still spans a finite period. Over this time, you'll have multiple careers (concurrent or sequential) and numerous jobs.

Despite what you may think, it isn't too soon to identify your long-term professional desires and what you should be doing now to achieve them, particularly if your organization and role are changing. Here, you'll consider your motivation, your likes and dislikes, your skills and competencies, and your desired legacy.

You can find some reflective questions in Appendix A, "Career Reflections," which is available on the book's Web site.

Implications

Yogi Berra, baseball immortal, is credited with saying, "When you come to a fork in the road, take it." When it comes to career options, Yogi would likely add that education, progressive experience, proficient functional skills, and a good network should increase the number of "forks" coming your way. The probability for making the right choice in employment matters increases exponentially when you have more information and personal awareness.

TRUTH

4

Teaching long division doesn't work on a Blackberry

A Wall Street executive recently confided that she was losing the battle of "balance" in her life. Her commute to downtown Manhattan was beyond taxing, and her job, despite her boss's promises otherwise, called for far too many hours and most of her weekends.

As if things on the home front weren't troubled enough, it finally came to a head late one night when she realized that she was trying to teach her fifth-grade son how to do his math homework from her Blackberry.

You can't add full value at work if you're directly or indirectly creating havoc at home. You also can't have a life if you're too busy making a living.

Whether you're new to or a veteran of managerial responsibilities, your learning curve in the "better, faster, and cheaper world" is getting steeper. And it needs to be. Changes brought on by fierce global competition, real-time market shifts, increasing regulation, and demanding stockholders are causing calendar pages to turn in an eye's blink. Consequently, long hours (though hopefully not like what is described in this Truth) have become more of the norm, and your personal support system—more so than ever—plays a critical role in determining your success.

Before you say "yes" to the new or expanded assignment, be sure you have the support and commitment of your family and the network you rely on.

At home, given the time and attention that you'll be devoting to managing organizational change—particularly in its early phases—there is bound to be stress and disruption. This may lead to unhappiness and resentment. Your goal is to ease everyone's burden to the extent possible. Talk about the worst-case expectations for your commitment, and why and how everyone can be supportive. Pledge to stay in touch with the feelings of your spouse and family. Try to resolve differences as they occur, without letting them fester.

> Your personal support system—more so than ever—plays a critical role in determining your success.

Make the most of your quality time together with new and familiar activities. Friends and extended family members may be able to help in the short term. Perhaps other resources are available. If you're relocating, be sensitive to the timing of the move, especially if children are involved, and the need to quickly get acquainted with the new environment.

In terms of your professional network, you'll need help—and you should not be shy about asking. No leader can do it all. Refresh or develop a small team of trusted advisors within and outside the organization to share your observations, and compare experiences. These people can fall into one of three professional categories: technical advisors, cultural interpreters, and political counselors.

Technical advisors provide expertise, analysis, and insight into available resources, strategy, and markets. They're treasures of information. They can provide you with tools and applications that will keep you abreast of operational hiccups and efficiencies in real-time.

> Develop a small team of trusted advisors within and outside the organization to share your observations, keep your point of view, and compare experiences.

Cultural interpreters help you understand your organizational landscape and how to best adapt to it. They provide insight into the culture, norms, rites, customs, and assumptions. They help you speak the language of the new company.

Political counselors help you understand your key organizational relationships. They provide advice and act as a sounding board for your change agenda. They provide suggestions on how to implement your ideas and challenge you with "what if" questions.

Be sure to have a good mix of these advisors to provide you the balance of perspective.

TRUTH

5

It's not what you've got;
it's what you need

Rodger had impressive academic credentials, including an advanced degree from one of the country's leading business schools. There, he learned how to slice and dice balance sheets, examine income statements, and perform business analysis—skills that are great tools for anyone at any stage of a business career.

He graduated at the top of his class and had a choice of employers. He joined the ABC Company and was soon identified as a person with "high potential." He was given challenging assignments that had direct impact on the company's future strategic positioning, and he was given a staff to help him in these endeavors. He quickly established himself as a functional expert.

Unfortunately for Rodger, he also had an Achilles heel that became more and more visible over time. His inability to manage conflicting interests within his team became a liability.

Although this matter is being addressed, many of our finest educational institutions continue to fall short when it comes to teaching their students the correlating "people" skills and competencies for business—failing to supplement business theory with the practical managerial guidance that allows them to lead and engage others through workplace change. Don't let this happen to you.

As you manage the required shift of your organization's new direction, you'll be adjusting your team's strategy, people, and processes to keep up with or get ahead of the latest business wave or technological avalanche. You may meet many of these challenges with your inherent skills, but others will require time and attention to come to fruition.

Organizations differ widely in how they provide a supportive framework and the necessary resources for addressing areas for professional development, particularly the management of change. But don't fret if your company doesn't have deep pockets for training, generous tuition reimbursement, or a learning center. You're better off knowing "a lot about a little" than "a little about a lot," because research tells us there are certain skills, among many, that can spell the difference between your managerial success and failure.

Skills are task-oriented, involving knowledge transfer and measurable behavioral modification. They involve ability, and they may be learned in a classroom or at a seminar. For managing change, you need both analytical and execution skills.

Analytical skills are gleaned from any MBA textbook. These skills involve your ability to analyze the current state of organizational affairs—that is, people, processes, systems, finances, and structure—against what you deem to be a more desirable endpoint. This involves troubleshooting, identifying gaps, analyzing root causes, and identifying the possible courses of action.

Execution skills are where the managerial rubber hits the road. These skills involve your ability to relate to your team and to determine what intervention method to utilize to make the required changes.

You need to be proficient at these skills:

- **Envisioning**—Your ability to determine that ideal organizational end state and to communicate it to others.

- **Inventiveness**—Your ability to think of numerous nonobvious and creative ways of getting things done.

- **Negotiation**—Your ability to work persistently and constructively with colleagues to secure resources or assistance that is needed to support the team.

- **Decision making**—Your ability to choose among multiple courses of action with certainty, using all perspectives and data available.

- **Teaching**—Your ability to help a team member learn experientially.

- **Interpersonal skills**—Your ability to communicate, listen, confront, persuade, and generally work constructively with others, particularly in challenging conditions.

Research tells us there are certain skills, among many, that can spell the difference between your managerial success and failure.

■ **Implementation skills**—Your ability to introduce or refine processes that generate the desired results.

Training in these skills is easily accessible and relatively adaptable. It's also cost effective. You'll explore all these skills throughout the rest of this book.

TRUTH

6

To manage change, you must lead change

In the organizational setting of years gone by, most managers spent their time on the tasks and processes associated with planning, organizing, controlling, staffing, coordinating, and troubleshooting.

In today's dynamic business world, you still have these traditional responsibilities; however, you must also juggle the multiple complexities and options for making your world "better, faster, and cheaper." To be an effective manager, you must be an effective leader—a leader of transformation!

Why is this critical? Research tells us that successful organizational transformation is 70 to 90 percent based on leadership and only 10 to 30 percent on management.

Most people think they know what leadership is. It *looks like* the confident business head at the podium, the politician greeting constituents, someone advancing a social cause, or the captain of the ship plotting a new direction. Winston Churchill, Mahatma Gandhi, and Eleanor Roosevelt come to mind. It *sounds like*, "I have a dream," or "Mr. Gorbachev, take down this wall!"

In its most simplistic form, leadership is your ability to compel people to act in a complementary manner that accomplishes desirable organizational goals with integrity and respect. It's the enabler that allows you to get things done with and through your team. It pulls people as opposed to pushing them. It's the steady and confident force behind the organization's transformation.

> Successful organizational transformation is 70 to 90 percent based on leadership and only 10 to 30 percent on management.

Leadership's professional traits include high confidence and deliberation, low anxiety, and an ability to motivate.

Its personal attributes include care, fortitude, perseverance, intelligence, nurturance, and sound judgment.

Its style is flexible, adaptable to people and circumstance.

Its tasks include conflict resolution, persuasion, decision making, social relations, and teaching.

Its behaviors include welcoming new ideas, managing information, integrating people, building community, and managing productivity.

Its approach includes rallying, rebellion, and taking charge.

A leader's job description has five major components for you to consider and master. The first responsibility of leadership involves your ability to create a vision. A vision identifies the organization's desired end-state. It gives people a direction and a goal. It motivates and inspires people to a common cause, and it builds organizational unity. It enables people to build linkage between their activities and how they contribute to the greater good.

Second, leaders cultivate a desirable culture. Through your words and actions, you set the tone for the organization. Your words must convey confidence, respect, and authority; your actions must be reflective of the organization's values, characterized with honesty and integrity. Your zeal and energy can serve as a benchmark for your team. Your style must be open, and it should welcome all perspectives. You also need to instill a sense of urgency.

Third, leadership is about allocating limited resources—financial and human. As much as you want to give everyone a blank check or an endless supply of personnel requisitions as they leave your office, reality dictates that you play the role of tiebreaker when it comes to competing interests. You need analytical skills, as well as a team-building focus to keep everyone dedicated to "bigger picture" concerns versus parochial temptations.

Fourth, leaders communicate. You not only need to "walk the talk" but also you need to "talk the talk." Your communications efforts must "connect" with your team, conveying your vision and reinforcing your organizational values at every opportunity.

Last, leaders get targeted results. Ask any former manager of the New York Yankees, and he'll tell you that wins are nice (and necessary) during the regular season, but victories in the playoffs and World Series rings are what count. This holds true for corporate America as well.

While no one realistically expects you to be the next Eleanor Roosevelt or Mahatma Gandhi, your team likely has high standards to which you're held. Your efforts to provide direction and to compel them to act can be the key barometer for your future.

TRUTH

7

You can't do without a "can-do" attitude

As you engage with your team, you'll ask for their patience and speed, passion and love, and devotion and sacrifice. You'll ask for their ideas and suggestions. You'll ask them to consider new and different ways of getting their jobs done. You'll ask them to take initiative and accountability for problem solving. You'll ask them to test everything they're told. You'll ask them to scrutinize, identify, and live values. You'll ask them to use both sides of their brain—logic and creativity. You'll ask them to build the link between their job and the organization's bottom line. You'll ask them to spend their waking moments contemplating "better, faster, and cheaper" ways to complete the tasks at hand.

With a list so daunting of requests, you can't expect your team to change its approach to work if you don't consider your own.

That's where you can make a *big* difference.

Attitudes are everything! In fact, it may surprise you to know research shows that how your attitude is conveyed and perceived has a powerful influence on your team—making it one of the most powerful levers available to drive organizational change.

No one should be more enthusiastic, energized, and excited about the task at hand than you. By example, you set the bar—for yourself and others. You drive your team's motivation and commitment to the cause. You're the root cause of other's inspiration. The glass is always half full, and your attitude must be nothing short of "can-do!"—even if storm clouds gather.

When Samuel Walton, founder of Wal-Mart, opened his second store in 1964 in Harrison, Arkansas, the first day was a disaster with 115-degree heat. Manure came into the store from donkey rides, watermelons popped in the heat, and you can imagine the testy and impatient temperament of those who emerged. One local critic called it, "the worst retail store I've ever seen."

> Research shows that how your attitude is conveyed and perceived has a powerful influence upon your team.

While other people may have thrown in the towel, Walton learned from this unfortunate event on the way to building a retail empire.

There are many other examples of those who continually kept a positive view despite the obstacles. Abe Lincoln was defeated in six elections before becoming president; Albert Einstein failed math in his youth; Ted Turner scoffed critics who said there was no audience for CNN; USA Today is more widely read today than ever, despite early market skepticism; Amazon continues to keep UPS busy, despite early projections that an online book supplier wasn't a viable business model; and Hillary Clinton has persevered, even with her detractors.

How do you make your optimism contagious? Listen. When a person voices some level of dissatisfaction or helplessness—that is, "You can't fight city hall," or "Anyone else they would let slide"— they're expressing blame, conflict, or rejection, or they're feeling misunderstood or victimized.

To address this negativity, you have to convert the person's new attitude into desirable direction and action.

Exhale and reflect before you share your thoughts. Though easier said than done, try to avoid defensiveness, and allow the person to express her concerns. Try to determine the root cause of the negativity. Show how her attitude is limiting, what its individual and collective consequences are, and why she must modify it. Explain the benefits of viewing the issue from multiple perspectives. Make her feel relevant. Try to offer choices that allow for some control over her destiny. There is probably a silver lining to the matter at hand, as well as a way to frame the challenge in a positive manner that can provide comfort, reassurance, and consideration.

> To address negativity, you have to convert the person's new attitude into desirable direction and action.

And, no matter what, always keep your attitude positive!

TRUTH

8

If you don't stand for something, you'll fall for anything

Do you know the often-repeated difference between being "involved" and being "committed?" Think about your last ham and eggs breakfast—the chicken was involved; the pig was committed.

While it may not be the most pleasant visual, guess which animal you need to emulate?

Major organizational change doesn't happen by itself. It takes heart; it takes intellect; it takes passion and love; it takes integrity. It isn't something that you can do part time. It requires total commitment. It consumes your being.

Organizational change isn't about pontification; it's about action and delivery. It's about knocking down walls and overcoming inertia. It's about challenging the status quo. It's about standing up for what you believe.

A survey taken by the Society of Human Resource Management indicated that performance and character are the top two leadership behaviors and skills of importance. There is no greater test of performance and character than your ability to have courage during turbulent organizational times.

In May 1962, Russian President Nikita S. Khrushchev conceived the idea to up the ante in the Cold War by constructing a storage/launch site for intermediate range nuclear missiles in Cuba, a mere 90 miles from the U.S. coastline. With Fidel Castro's blessing, the warheads were quickly and quietly installed.

By October, President John F. Kennedy had been shown the photographic evidence from military reconnaissance that clearly delineated the missiles.

With such a nearby threat, JFK had a mandate for action, and he took it. While Soviet diplomats continued to deny the missiles' existence, JFK commenced an immediate flurry of correspondence between the two nuclear powers—including personal communications with Khrushchev. Clearly, JFK knew what was at stake,

> There is no greater test of performance and character than your ability to have courage during turbulent organizational times.

and he refused to bow to any Russian denials or demands. In an address to the American people, he outlined the nature of the threat, and true to his word, he ordered an immediate naval quarantine of Cuba, effectively blocking all shipments to and from the island. Finally, after a 7-day standoff, the Soviets ordered the missiles dismantled.

The whole affair—The Cuban Missile Crisis—was a direct threat to our national security, and JFK dealt with this test of his mettle in a straightforward, no-nonsense way. One can only imagine the tensions, anxieties, and pressures that were exerted on the inexperienced leader as he went through this ordeal. Surely, he must have lost sleep and been prone to second-guessing. However, he persevered. He didn't hide from the excruciating cerebral chess match; he seemingly welcomed every move.

This crisis marked JFK's emergence as a global leader who rose to the challenge and led the American people at a time when the alternatives were almost unthinkable.

Just because you won't be leading on a world stage doesn't mean you won't face comparable tests of character. Consider Sherron Watkins, the former vice president of corporate development for Enron.

In 2001, Ms. Watkins wrote an internal memo to Ken Lay, the company founder, detailing her concerns about the company's creative accounting methods. She warned that its improper practices were risky and that they might not withstand scrutiny. Her fear was that scandals were on the horizon absent immediate change.

History went on to prove that Ms. Watkins' revelations were correct, at the eventual cost of thousands of jobs and jail time for those who caused the corporate implosion.

Can you imagine how much stress and tension Ms. Watkins must have endured to raise this red flag? Yet she knew she had a moral, ethical, and professional duty to report the transgressions.

Like JFK and Ms. Watkins, keep your faith. Be consistent and predicable. Listen to your advisors. Let your values and your heart be your guiding forces.

Leadership isn't easy; its choices are hard. Don't let your backbone bend. The need for you to stand tall is imperative.

TRUTH

9

Run before you walk

You have just been hired, transferred, promoted, or had your responsibilities expanded to taking on and leading your team's change agenda. If this is a new or significantly modified assignment, chances are that an organizational announcement has been or will be distributed to all colleagues with the news. The announcement will include an overview of your background, the position's major responsibility areas, as well as an effective date.

If you wait until "day one" to start in your new role, you've waited too long.

> If you wait until "day one" to start in your new role, you've waited too long.

Effective managers know that in today's fast-paced business world, you want to hit the deck running. Therefore, before the pomp and circumstance of your "official" first day, you have a vested interest in surveying the landscape. Your goal is to gain a working familiarity—that will evolve into a working knowledge—about the business and your team as soon as possible.

To get started, you need a plan—specifically covering those first 90 days. Research tells us that there are some conceptual and practical adaptation strategies that you can tailor to your needs, which should get you off on solid footing.

- **Start fresh**—It's a new day. Throw out old mindsets. Don't believe that what worked yesterday will work today. Divorce yourself from the past. This is a new job with new responsibilities directing a new team. A clean slate approach is required.

- **Accelerate your on-the-job learning**—You need to get up to speed as quickly as possible. This means understanding markets, products, technologies, systems, stakeholders, politics, and the company's culture. Be organized in your approach. Review operating plans, performance data, and personnel records. Individually meet with all team members. Analyze key points of interface and processes. Look out for barriers. Interview customers and suppliers.

- **Diagnose the business challenges accurately—** Early and often, perform a SWOT analysis—listing the organization's strengths, weaknesses, opportunities, and threats. This can identify the rationale for why the organization must shift direction.

- **Secure early wins—**This can't be emphasized enough. Making a visible difference in a positive manner, early, can help build your credibility and create a sense on your team that the direction is proper. Define priorities and problematic areas (that is, a lack of urgency, teamwork, innovation, discipline, or focus). Concentrate on ways to add value and improve business results. Look for ways to engage in collective learning. Remember, your early actions will have a disproportionate influence on how you're perceived.

- **Negotiate success—**Build a productive relationship with your boss. No relationship is more critical for your success.

- **Achieve alignment—**Identify your vision, as well as the strategy and tactics necessary to accomplish the ends you want. Identify the values and desirable norms of behavior. Make sure that your organizational structure, core systems, and skills are optimal for what you're trying to accomplish. Channel energy in positive and predictable directions.

- **Begin to build your team—**You need to evaluate current staff and hire to fill gaps. Know the key opinion molders on your team, your team's perceived effectiveness, the demographics, the key capabilities and skills of each individual, turnover rates and reasons, and an overview of the existing culture. Discuss roles and interdependencies. Exploit every communications opportunity. Outline individual and collective performance measures. Displace those who don't fit into your new paradigm.

> Research tells us that there are some conceptual and practical adaptation strategies that you can tailor to your needs, which should get you off on solid footing.

- **Create coalitions**—Identify those key people who bring expertise, access to information, status, control of resources, and personal loyalty. Identify your supporters, your opponents, and those you need to convince. Determine how to bring your influence to bear.

- **Maintain your equilibrium**—Keep your perspective and priorities, and stay "connected." Don't overcommit. Embrace self-discipline. Set time aside for the hard work. Keep a work/family balance. The right-sounding boards are essential. Keep networking.

- **Expedite everyone**—Help get others acclimated to your speed and expectations.

By being cognizant of and following these strategies, you can touch all early bases, ensuring a successful transition into your new role.

TRUTH

10

Keep your boss your biggest fan

On "day one" of your assignment, your boss is your biggest fan. Your goal is to keep it that way!

One of the biggest mistakes people make in a job is trying to get to and stay in a "good place" with their boss, fearful of making waves. Subordinates often do this by adopting the role of corporate toady, wherein they "go along to get along"—reducing their role, presence, and impact to that of a rubber stamp or mimicking parrot.

While "getting along" is important, it's just a small part of what the boss is looking for. She wants you to faithfully serve and execute her agenda. And these expectations start on your first day.

> While "getting along" is important, it's just a small part of what the boss is looking for.

The challenge for you is to identify those expectations and to address the "gap" between those expectations and what you think you need to deliver. You must do this by gaining an early and ongoing understanding of five key discussion points.

The first point of discussion with your boss centers upon situational diagnostics. Here, you try to find out your boss's views of the organization—what's right and what's not? What's the organization's history? How did we get to this point? What makes this situation a challenge? Why is it unique? What behaviors are encouraged? How are those behaviors rewarded? What values are exemplified?

Your goal is to explore and see the world through your boss's eyes and not to be judgmental. Think of it as fact-finding.

The second topic is your responsibilities. What does your boss want you to accomplish in the first 30, 60, 90 days? Are there clear, measurable goals? How will you know that you have been successful? Are these timelines and goals realistic? Are there boundaries that you need to be aware of? Are there particular constituents with whom to build bridges or steer clear? Are there any team issues of significant consequence or sensitivity?

Third, it's important that you and your boss agree upon *how and how often you'll interface.* Specifically, what form of communication does your boss prefer? What kinds of operational issues does she want to be kept abreast of? How will surprises be eliminated or minimized? What types of decisions require consultation? Are weekly updates enough or too much? Are there particularly sensitive or politically charged matters that should be elevated sooner than later?

You'll also need to discuss resources. Beyond budget and headcount, what other resources are available? What role will your boss play in your acclimation? Will your boss be available to make introductions to key stakeholders? How involved does your boss want to be in sorting through some of the staffing issues? Will your boss help you champion the need for change?

Last, you should review how and how often you'll receive perform-ance feedback, and how this information may be used as the basis for your personal developmental plans.

These topics are listed in an order of logic and sequence. For example, you should be discussing situational diagnostics in your first conversation, but parameters concerning performance feedback are a topic you'll more likely evolve toward as your relationship becomes more comfortable over time.

TRUTH

11

There are only three ways to introduce change

In his thought-provoking book *The World Is Flat: A Brief History of the Twenty-First Century*, Thomas L. Friedman discusses the significant political, economic, demographic, technological, and social changes that have and are transpiring on a global basis, as well as their holistic impact. His premise (oversimplified here) is that these dynamic changes are causing our global landscape to become a bastion of local and regional neighborhoods, with former barriers of time, information, and distance all but removed.

How do these changes impact your business? How do they not?

Change is inevitable; it's perpetual, here, and real. And since change is going on outside your organization, you had best determine how you want to introduce and inculcate change within your team—at a minimum—to keep up.

Your options are threefold: force, persuasion, or education. Which to chose will likely be determined by what has to be done and how soon, recognizing that each method has advantages and limitations.

When is *force* applicable? Perhaps you just found out that Bill Gates is entering your industry tomorrow.

While it sounds harsh, you're in a situation where time isn't an ally. You'll find yourself in a dictatorial role, spending most of your time in your controller's office and mandating an overhaul of all business practices and processes.

While force will get the fastest results, its "ready, fire, aim!" practices will also cause the most casualties. People will grow to resent their lack of voice and the one-way communications. Hearts and minds will be lost due to your knee-jerk reactions.

By example, a Fortune 500 company, at the unyielding insistence of its CEO, hastily rolled out a new technology platform at its largest manufacturing site.

> Since change is going on outside your organization, you had best determine how you want to introduce and inculcate change within your team—at a minimum.

The results were absolutely devastating as the employees—absent sufficient training or communications—were uncertain of their new roles and accountabilities. In the confusion of the transition, they ran short of key raw materials, missed customer orders, and performed inventory control in a vacuum. The operation grinded to a halt, and time and money—well into seven figures—were wasted. Employee morale plummeted, deep scars resulted, and the facility took months to operationally recover.

Persuasion is a change management lever worth considering, but it's precarious. With this cultlike approach, you're relying upon your personal charisma, your expertise, your rebellion spirit ("us" versus "them"), or the exploitation of your personal relationships to sway opinion and drive organizational results. This can work when there are long-standing, trust-based associations and people look up to you. However, staying power may be limited unless it's based upon the conviction of purpose. To the downside, this approach will also take an extraordinary amount of personal investment and high-maintenance hand-holding.

If time and money permit, *education* is the ideal lever of change management. Here, you share with your team members the critical operational and financial information impacting the business, encouraging them to know and understand the organization's dollars and cents. You trust your employees and treat them as partners. You provide skills and personal effectiveness training. You assist them with anxiety and assist them with risk-taking. You empower your employees, share leadership, and create individual and collective learning opportunities as you progress through the change process. You attain a competitive edge through the growth and development of team members.

Education should also result in dividends such as a higher retention rate, as well as optimal employee engagement and productivity.

TRUTH

12

Build the case:
it's a challenge and
an opportunity

We have all seen the "Uncle Sam Wants You" posters encouraging military service.

If you were to design a similar recruiting advertisement for your team's participation in your change agenda, what would it look like? Would you use words and concepts such as *rewarding*, *learning journey*, *discovery*, *pride*, *innovation*, *empowering*, *freedom and latitude*, *hard work*, *continuous improvement*, or *fun*? Why would you select certain words versus others? Would your words capture and keep attention, set realistic expectations, and provide some level of inspiration?

Whether you're in a "startup" or a "turnaround," trying to change deeply rooted and outdated business practices and attitudes, or pushing the organization to "the next level," when you break the ice with your team about the change agenda, you not only want to make a good first impression, you also want to make a lasting one—one that you'll continually reinforce.

Your specific goals for this initial communication are twofold. First and foremost, paint a realistic picture about the challenges facing the business; second, encourage your team to join you in the journey toward optimal performance.

> You not only want to make a good first impression, you also want to make a lasting one.

Your key points must be succinct and focused. Tailored to your needs with appropriate detail, they should include the following.

- Driven by certain market, social, or economic factors identified in your SWOT analysis, the way that we presently approach and conduct our business must be put behind us. The status quo is, respectfully, dead.
- The cause for this change is inevitable. The organization's future viability is at stake.
- Our overall goals need to include improved quality, enhanced product or service offerings, reduced costs, optimal productivity, and the exploration and exploitation of new business development opportunities.

- As we begin our transformation, we need to create or validate an organization vision that defines a clear sense of purpose, including an explanation and articulation of why we're here and the critical path to this end.

- Related strategic objectives need to be developed. These identify the key things that must be accomplished to make the vision a reality.

- Functional/departmental tactics and individual performance measures need to be developed to guide and assist us with how we can accomplish our strategic goals.

- Organizational values and desirable behaviors need to be identified, outlining how we're going to conduct our operations and business—that is, by leading visibly and vigorously, being decisive, having the courage to act, creating a "safe to say" environment, aligning authority with responsibility, pursuing excellence, and so on.

- The desirable results from these efforts need to be identified. Progress shall be tracked.

- All parts of our business will be participating in this transform-ation. There are no sacred cows. Every product, process, policy, and work practice needs to be examined. Everyone's roles and contributions must be analyzed. Bring forth the best elements of the present and couple them with an innovative future.

- This requires hard work and sacrifice. We need to embrace a sense of urgency. Our mantra is "better, faster, and cheaper."

- This is an opportunity to actively participate—in the creation of our future.

- This requires "all hands on deck." Everyone must be involved.

- We will be stronger—individually and collectively. New ideas, suggestions and innovative ways of thinking are welcomed. Through this unique opportunity, we can learn new skills and new things about each other and ourselves.

Deliver your points in a confident and calming manner. conveying your unbridled enthusiasm. Make your points personal to the extent possible, and use words such as *we* and *us*, not *you* and *they*.

TRUTH

13

Teach others how to treat you

Have you wondered why a 12- year-old child will rebel at a directive by one parent but generally be hushed and compliant when it comes to the other? At the risk of playing psychologist, it's because we have, directly or indirectly, taught our children where, when, and how to push the envelope. The question is, "Are adults any different?"

The answer is a resounding "No."

During times of rapid organizational change, it's imperative that you get everyone "on the same page" at the onset, alleviating any potential anxiety or frustration. To do this, you must identify—and be prepared to live and enforce—some basic rules or "suggestions" regarding your team's attitudes and behaviors.

While every situation will be different, here are some practical guidelines for speaking to your team about how you will treat them:

> It's imperative that you get everyone "on the same page" at the onset, alleviating any potential anxiety or frustration.

- You'll trust everyone until they give you a reason not to. Everyone is starting with a blank slate.

- You're available "24/7," though hopefully, that doesn't need to be tested too often.

- Their needs are important, and you'll do everything in your power to assist them with obtaining the needed resources.

- You're here to help, listen, observe, and learn. You aren't afraid of rolling up your sleeves. You'll make decisions as quickly and efficiently as possible if there are limited or competing resources.

- To the extent possible, everyone will have a voice.

- You'll provide general direction and give feedback on a timely basis.

- When mistakes are made, you'll use them as opportunities for collective learning.

- You'll never embarrass anyone. Counseling matters will be addressed behind closed doors.

- Confidentiality shall be maintained to the extent possible.

- There are no guarantees for employment, but participating in this change agenda with you can enhance everyone's employability. Roles will likely change and grow; skills will be developed and enhanced. Rewards will be considered.

- You'll keep everyone up-to-date regarding organizational progress and key initiatives. Regular staff meetings will be held, and "ad hoc" as needed.

- You believe in the future. You're looking forward to this journey of exploration. You shall try to create a climate that fosters the sharing of ideas.

Here are some practical guidelines to communicate to your team about how you expect to be treated, and how you hope they will interact with each other:

- Everyone is to be treated with respect.

- Appreciate everyone's contribution.

- Be punctual. Meetings start on time. Be prepared.

- Make sure deliverables meet commitments.

- Failing to communicate isn't an acceptable excuse. If delays are anticipated or significant road blacks encountered, you want to hear about it as soon as possible. Surprises aren't welcome.

- Be aware that we may evolve to an "ask for forgiveness, not permission" model, but that's not where we're starting. You expect to be kept informed of the status of all key projects.

- Work hard and work smart. Maintain professionalism at all times. Everything you do is a reflection on the team.

- Bring problems to management's attention on a timely basis. Even more so, bring solutions.

- Don't have selfish goals and parochial interests. This must be a team effort.

- Treat each other as adults. Address problems and resolve conflict at the appropriate levels. Only get others involved or escalate the matter if necessary.

- If there are any concerns, tell management about them first. The water cooler isn't the place for hearsay or the airing of dirty laundry.

- Know that, in time, everyone will have the opportunity to create his own job descriptions and work processes. Innovation is encouraged.

- Don't walk into management's office without a recommendation for handling the concern being raised.

- Understand that management is looking for and assessing employees' commitment, contribution, and collaboration.

TRUTH

14

If you don't know where
you're going,
you won't get there

It might surprise you to know that with a few words, your team will likely experience higher job satisfaction, motivation, commitment, loyalty, pride, and productivity.

What words could generate such resounding results?

The answer is your vision. And if effectively developed and communicated—addressing the broader organizational questions, "Why are we here?" and "Why is it important that we're here?"—it can move mountains.

Early in his presidency, John F. Kennedy shared his vision for the U.S. space program by challenging the scientific community to reach the moon before the turn of the decade. While his proclamation had its skeptics, the message galvanized the scientific community around this unprecedented picture of the future.

When leaders articulate a vision in this manner, it serves four key purposes. First, it clarifies, articulates, and defines the purpose of the entire organization. Second, it serves as a motivator and a directional beacon for all followers. Third, the words implicitly or explicitly prompt people to action through their desire for affiliation with a noble cause. Fourth, it invites feedback that can be evaluated and processed.

Whether you're creating or revitalizing an organization—a manufacturing site, shipping department, service call center, or local bank branch—*you need to have a vision.*

An effective vision has several unique characteristics. It must be compelling and plausible, as it must

You need to have a vision.

be translated into organizational realities. It must allow followers to imagine the desired future state of the enterprise, serving the long-term interests of all constituents. It must have focus such that followers will understand it as the basis for all future decision making. It must be relatively simple, easy to communicate, and easy to explain. It must be ambitious and inspirational, having both intellectual and emotional appeal.

It may focus upon excellence, industry leadership, continuous improvement, quality of life enhancements, noble cause, societal responsibility, stakeholder values, and be customer-centric.

Vision statements need to be the reason that you get out of bed in the morning.

To commence a collective dialogue and provoke thought about an "ideal" organizational vision statement, there are several worthy considerations; two are exemplary.

First, in their book *Competing for the Future*, Hamel and Prahalad outline a series of conceptual questions for organizational leaders to consider when pondering the future state of their markets and organizations. These include contemplating tomorrow around what customers you'll serve, the channels that you'll reach them through, the competitive landscape, the basis of your competitive advantage, the source of your sales and margins, and the identification of the product, services, or technological capability that will make your organization unique.

Second, in *Good to Great*, Jim Collins referred to the "Hedgehog" concept, suggesting that great companies have a deep understanding of the concerns around "What are you deeply passionate about?" "What you can be the best in the world at?" and "What drives your economic engine?"

The intersection of these differentiating questions is the essence of defining your organization's vision.

Don't underestimate the time and effort required to develop a vision statement. It's hard work, requires teamwork and consensus-building, and you must involve the right people. At the most senior levels in larger organizations, identifying a vision statement usually falls upon the shoulders of the CEO and the executive committee, who then take it to the board of directors for discussion, editing, and approval.

You are your CEO and the decision maker of your team. Get the opinions of your key constituents. Use a facilitator if necessary to keep the discussion on track. If helpful, get the reactions of a focus group of employees (or the like; preferably opinion molders). You may obtain some terrific input.

You can find some examples of vision statements in Appendix B, "Vision/Mission Statements," available for download on the book's Web site.

TRUTH

15

To realize the future, you must create it

Once you know your destination, you will need a map to get there. Therefore, while you have those people around the table discussing your organization's vision, don't be in a rush to adjourn. Making your dream a reality requires strategy.

This is where pragmatic business planning begins.

Reflecting upon your new or revitalized vision, you should consider whether your organization has the appropriate resources and competencies or whether it needs different skills, systems enhancements, better information, different market participation, or alternate financing models. Strategy considers your present organizational state as baseline and outlines the course to where you want to be. It addresses and identifies the "gap" between the two organizational states by answering, "What must we accomplish?" for the vision to be realized.

Like the vision statement, your strategy is forward looking. It should be internally focused and provide consensus-driven, goal-oriented guidance with a 12- to 30-month outlook. It should be clear and concise, describing how the organization will relate to and respond to its environment. It should be inspirational, compelling, and plausible. As the first level of detail for your business plan, it should also be easy to understand and to communicate.

Strategy is usually stated in the form of specific objectives that are measurable and time bound, contemplating the financial and operating results and return expectations required. These objectives are generally categorized as "critical" or "subordinate" in nature.

The level of detail in each objective will vary to your comfort level, but the direction, timeframe, and deliverables should be clear.

Begin your discussion about strategy by focusing on what it takes to make your vision a reality. Don't aim for modest improvement; take a good "stretch," but stay realistic and focused. The power of strategy, especially in changing times, is derived from its ability to direct employees' actions, secure their commitment, and allocate people and financial resources accordingly to your competitive advantage. You'll find that having a few meaningful and prioritized strategic objectives in each of the applicable categories that follow is highly motivational, and it's far better than drowning in detail.

For **markets and customers**, you may want to consider ways to further penetrate and grow existing markets or target new ones through mergers, acquisitions, forward or reverse integration, in- or out-licensing, and strategic alliances. Also, based on the data collected, consider exit strategies and outsourcing for the low-performing aspects of your businesses.

Customers and funding sources are the lifeblood of any business. The relationships with your customers—internal or external—should be a partnership. You should continually be providing compelling reasons for your customers to do business with you—not only by satisfying their needs, but also by anticipating their needs. You need to be linked to your customer through your people, your performance, and your information.

> The power of strategy...is derived from its ability to direct employees' actions, secure their commitment, and allocate people and financial resources accordingly to your competitive advantage.

For **products and services**, identify strategic objectives to meet the needs of present customers/clients, as well as to differentiate or add unique value to the organization's future offerings (such as quality, speed, price, technology, innovation, and other product/service applications).

For **business processes**, consider more effective and efficient ways to address the organization's cost of inventory and finished goods storage, work-in-progress, the need for quality and reduced service call rates or defects, the time and effort required for material or process changeovers, regulatory interactions, project management, resource allocations, or options for enhanced distribution.

For **people and reward systems**, you may need to obtain or enhance competencies for general management, sales and marketing, technology, customer service, research and development, distribution, or quality. Also, you need to assess and upgrade your current approach to attracting, selecting, motivating, and retaining talent. Consider options for protecting intellectual property. Look for some of the warning signs, such as turnover, productivity downturns, high turnover or absenteeism, and the like to flag potential trouble areas.

For **structure and facilities**, the driving force behind any change in organizational structure will likely depend on how you align your business with your customers and how much empowerment you provide to your employees (discussed later in Truth 26, "Even if it hurts, take your fingers off the steering wheel"). In this regard, an external perspective is encouraged.

For **technologies**, you must examine new ways of tracking initiatives and information and measuring performance.

You can find some examples of strategic objectives in Appendix C, "Strategic Objectives," available for download on the book's Web site.

TRUTH

16

Convert aspiration to invitation

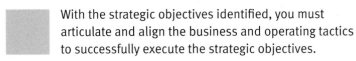 With the strategic objectives identified, you must articulate and align the business and operating tactics to successfully execute the strategic objectives.

This is when you need to roll up your sleeves and get more people involved.

Tactics are the short-term action steps (generally within a 6- to 12-month period) that identify "how" your resources—financial, human, and technical—will be assigned, allocated, and deployed within the organization to implement and achieve the strategic objectives. They're generally identified at a functional level. They cite the specific activities, changes, accountabilities, and deadlines required.

Tactics will also form the basis for future individual performance planning, as well as the identification of roles and accountabilities. Your management of this tactical creation process and its subsequent guidance is critical from several perspectives.

First, despite what may be your inclination otherwise, you most likely need to have the input of a broader audience—those closest to the work and most respected by your team. Research indicates that involving stakeholders directly in the problem-solving, knowledge sharing, and examining of the progress and challenges of the change effort always yields a better result. You must give your team an invitation to express their initiative, innovation, and ingenuity on the path to enduring, positive change. You must also tell them—upfront and with honest feedback—how their input will or won't be used. You want your team to experience the energy and pride derived from creating its goals and aspirations.

Second, you want to establish a scenario where you can demonstrate some tangible, quick "wins." This can help keep people engaged and enthusiastic about the change process and ensure all stakeholders that progress is being made. This also reinforces your desired sense of urgency.

Third, you need to be sure that the tactics are aligned and not at cross-purposes. This involves macro-level coordination. Focus on the desired results through a reconciliation, harmonization, and integration of selfish and competing interests. Slay the sacred cows, knock down the silos, fight the parochial interests, and end programs that aren't giving you the required return. Include the voice of your key customers and suppliers, allowing them a voice through shared perspective, as they will make a terrific sounding board.

Last, remember that your resources are limited. Rome wasn't built in a day. If you try to do "everything" as a priority, there's a good chance that you'll disappoint. For example, the pace at which organizational leadership addresses technology needs, reorganizes the sales territories, or integrates the R&D function will vary due to budget, complexity, and relationships with key constituents.

Research indicates that involving stakeholders directly in the problem-solving, knowledge sharing, and examining of the progress and challenges of the change effort always yields a better result.

You can find some examples of tactics in Appendix D, "Tactics," available on the book's Web site.

17

Having organizational
values matters;
living them means more

Contrary to what may seem common sense, it isn't important what values your organization identifies; it's important that your organization has values. (To add a qualifier, your organization has to have the "right" values—as opposed to what values the Ku Klux Klan might embrace.)

Why?

Organizational values have a holistic impact

Values are deeply rooted and constant over time. They're composed of and evidenced by customs, rites, and symbols. In an organizational setting, they're reflected in policies and procedures, dress code, hours of work, employee relations practices, communications patterns, rules for corporate governance, and the environmental setting.

> It isn't important what values your organization identifies; it's important that your organization has values.

You can see an example of how values holistically impact an organization on the television show *The Apprentice*. Watch the boardroom scene at the end of each show. The room is dark; participants are instructed when to enter; the furniture appears to be solid mahogany; the décor is formal; the table is long; the chair that Donald Trump sits in is in the center of all activity, and it's larger than the others; he enters through a private door; and he's addressed as "Mr. Trump." These environmental factors alone tell boardroom visitors much about this organization's values.

Values are the basis of community

As pointed out by Jody Hoffer Gittell in her book that analyzed the people strategies associated with one company's unparalleled success, *The Southwest Airlines Way*, "Relationships shape our own personal identities; they define who we are. It's no wonder, then, that relationships among people who work together—particularly their shared goals, shared knowledge, and respect for one another, or lack thereof—are such powerful drivers of organizational performance."

Values define relationships: they're the link to your team

Among other benefits, values foster individual and collective "connectivity" between people, promote loyalty, define acceptable attitudes, and encourage ethics. They're the fundamental underpinning for determining acceptable norms of conduct. They allow team members to consider and define their respective self-definition.

Values are a required managerial competency

Evidence suggests that your success as a leader is based, to a large degree, on your ability to identify and clarify values, communicate them, and harmoniously align your strategies and business practices.

Values are a critical aspect of organizational viability

In *Built to Last*, Stanford University professors James Collins and Jerry Porras analyzed industrial leaders such as Merck, Sony, Wal-Mart, 3M, Disney, and IBM, as well as some of these companies' less than successful competitors, to identify the differentiating organizational characteristics for success. They discovered, among several key findings, that what made these companies enduring, prosperous, and preeminent was a *core ideology*—a set of values and purpose fundamental to the company that seldom, if ever, changed.

Other studies have likewise concluded that strong corporate cultures based on shared values have outperformed other firms by huge margins.

The key to values identification is enforcement

If you aren't prepared to act upon your values, you're better off not having any.

Research has shown that *values-less leadership*—the disparity of values between management and the employees—as well as a lack of management commitment to the organization's values are two of the leading reasons for reduced employee job satisfaction.

Values aren't negotiable. They should be considered as the litmus test for all organizational behavior and discipline.

Get started

If your team or organization doesn't have a highly visible, well-articulated values proposition, you should act accordingly. To get started, you should use a participatory approach, identifying whatever values and behaviors you aspire for. To the extent possible, they should be concise, readily understandable, universal in application, consensus-driven, and customized for your organization.

You can find examples of values statements in Appendix E, "Values," available on the book's Web site.

On an ongoing basis

As you tend to view and interpret the world around you through your own values, you should

- Make values clear.
- Express values in behavioral terms so they're recognizable and can be emulated.
- Enable teams to frame specific values for that team, its customers, and its outputs.
- Provide mechanisms to keep values visible.
- Incorporate values into business planning, performance management, and compensation practices.
- Provide values feedback to each person.
- Provide training.

TRUTH

18

Make the change agenda everyone's agenda

Ever wonder why people will be enthusiastic about a sports team, religious affiliation, or political party that they have no real influence or impact for, but these same folks can't muster a modicum of passion about the source of their paycheck?

Research shows that you not only have a professional interest in having your team on board, but a personal one.

In *Geeks & Geezers*, Bennis and Thomas examined several cases of leadership failures by analyzing the records of short-tenured CEOs, including Coca-Cola's Douglas Invester, Compaq's Eckhard Pfeiffer, Cerner's Neal Patterson, P&G's Durk Jager, and Warnaco's Linda Wachler. In their findings, the authors concluded that these "crash and burns" weren't due to a lack of professional business competence; rather, the derailments were, in part or directly, due to the leader's failure to motivate and inspire support for their respective agenda.

Unless you want to experience a career hiccup, you must involve the entire organization in the process of change. To this end, you can embrace several "best practices."

- You must personally demonstrate commitment. Show your team that you're in it for the long haul through your hard work, patience, and fortitude. This isn't about resume fodder.

> You must involve the entire organization in the process of change.

- You need to speak about and reinforce the organization's vision at every opportunity. Never let it become "out of sight, out of mind."

- The organization's values proposition must be fully integrated into the cultural fabric of the enterprise.

- You need to break your business plan into doable parts and let people see, experience, and share in the progress.

- To the extent possible, you need to make the change effort "holistic" by creating organizational conditions that foster "bottom-up" participation. Challenge people to think about team and individual goals and the input, throughput, and output required. Do it to ensure related quality and speed.

■ You need to make the change agenda personal by helping people understand how they're part of the organization and explaining how and why they should act in those interests.

■ You must be sure to view change from the perspective of all stakeholders. To the extent required, secure their "buy-in" by demonstrating why the change agenda is in their vested interest.

■ You need to constantly update people about the "big picture" of the organization, as well as constantly monitor your organization's key performance indicators and workplace climate.

■ From time to time, you need to "float a trial balloon" with other stakeholders concerning some of the bigger changes being contemplated.

A CEO once asked her HR director to rack up some frequent flyer miles in a hurry by visiting seven cities spread across the United States in two days. The purpose of the trip was to confidentially "test the waters" about a significant organizational change that she was contemplating. Ultimately, the feedback was so negative that the idea was abandoned, and hindsight proved the decision to be the correct one.

■ You need to keep your message visible. Your vision, strategy, tactics, and values should be on screen savers, coffee mugs, mouse pads, and framed in conference rooms.

■ You can make it fun!

In rolling out a new quality policy in a manufacturing facility, the management team, among other efforts, placed "quality scoreboards" throughout the plant; embossed the new quality slogan on its stationery, posted it in high-traffic areas, and printed it on sweatshirts; and ran contests recognizing and rewarding significant contributions. The result was an increase in employee awareness and participation, a heightened sense of common purpose ("connectivity"), and a quantifiable improvement in the facility's overall quality performance.

■ To reinforce your message, you may want or need to do something symbolic.

In *The CEO and the Monk: One Company's Journey to Profit and Purpose* (2004), coauthors Robert Catell, Kenny Moore, and Glenn Rifkin describe the corporate funeral that was held at KeySpan to visibly and respectfully acknowledge a closure of the former ways that the enterprise conducted its business. The company's top 400 managers attended the ceremony, held in 1994, and it's still referred to by those with tenure as part of the lore of the company.

A funeral may seem a bit drastic; getting everyone involved with the message isn't.

TRUTH

19

We listen with our eyes

Have you ever sat in on a presentation where the speaker's message became lost due to his fidgeting posture, soft monotone, or lack of eye contact? The good news is that you need not make the same mistake.

In his book *Silent Messages*, Dr. Albert Mehrabian divides human communication skills into three areas that we must be cognizant of: verbals, vocals, and nonverbals. For communication to be most effective and efficient, there must be congruence across these factors as heard and observed by your audience.

Verbals

Intuition might lead you to believe that our spoken words, our verbals, are of most influence when it comes to conveying our point of view; after all, our language reflects our upbringing, education, status, and intelligence. However, our verbals *aren't* the most influential. Research tells us that through our own biases and filters, as well as our natural tendency to synthesize information into digestible, easy-to-understand pieces, only a small percent of our words hit their intended mark.

As a quick test of this theorem, think of the last presidential State of the Union address that you heard. Chances are that the rhetoric is well beyond memory, but a few headlines may remain.

> Only a small percent of our words hit their intended mark.

Vocals

Beyond words, the tone of our voice, our *vocals*, communicates a greater portion of our message. This refers to our volume and inflections. For example, sarcasm, a harsh or belittling tone, a raised voice, and warmth are all directly associated with the receiver's interpretation of your message.

Just ask the recently scolded child if the words or the volume of the reprimand caught her attention!

Nonverbals

Of most significance are our nonverbal indicators. Here, our body language—posture, "presence," gestures, facial expressions, and eye contact—communicate a majority of what we are trying to say. The extension of your finger, the shaking of your head, or your dramatic pound on the desk sends a clear nonverbal signal to your audience about your emphasis or agreement—almost eight times more so than your words.

Richard Nixon experienced an example of ill-intentioned and unfortunate nonverbal communications. In a televised 1960 presidential debate, wilting under the stage's bright lights, his public persona was significantly damaged as the national audience focused more upon his physical discomfort than the words he was trying to express.

What are the pragmatic implications of this when you're discussing change management with your colleagues? Consistency of message!

Recognizing what may be the limitations of verbal capabilities, clearly outline the rationale for change—in a manner that creates the realization of new realities, reduces confusion and chaos, and welcomes exploration and new thinking. This explanation must be repeatedly delivered—day after day—and predicated upon honesty. It should outline the basis for action in a compelling manner that allows for realistic expectations about the future state of the organization.

In setting your vocal tone about the change agenda, you must demonstrate care and empathy in a manner that will be seen as a persuasive invitation to jump on, stay on, or lead the bandwagon. You don't need flash and sizzle; you need logic. Deliver your words from the heart with a little fire and brimstone, in a JFK-like "ask not what your organization can do for you, but what you can do for your organization" manner, ultimately seeking individual participation, while instilling a sense of shared team pride.

In attempting to maximize the likelihood that "message sent" equals "message received," be wary of your nonverbal behaviors. Stand tall, exude confidence, lean forward, and connect with your audience in all interactions. And if your introverted side tries to rise, counter it with practice. For, just as you would not go to a meeting, conduct a sales call, or make a major presentation without rehearsal, nor should you here.

Be wary of your nonverbal behaviors.

When you communicate your thoughts and understanding of complex business challenges in a way that resonates with your listeners and ensures congruence of your words, tone, and nonverbal signals, you won't need a second chance to make a first impression.

TRUTH

20

Email is the tool of the devil

People get nervous when the organizational grapevine begins to buzz about potential acquisitions/takeovers, major process enhancements, facility closures, operational shifts, or a reduction in force. Reactions can take on several forms—from hushed water cooler conversation to sabotage or even violence.

To mitigate your team's concerns, you need to be a proactive communicator. But being proactive alone doesn't guarantee effectiveness.

Recognizing that there is no such thing as the perfect sharing of meaning and understanding, it's up to you to determine the appropriate content of your message, as well as the best medium through which you should convey your thoughts to your many stakeholders.

First, to effectively communicate, you must solicit and understand the needs of your audience.

- You want your organization's top management to comprehend and fully support your efforts. Be crisp, polished, and focused in your communications. You're telling and selling. You need top management's sponsorship and cheerleading. They can help you with budget, knock down silos, initiate broader systemic changes, and grant you access to information and people that might otherwise be off limits. They need to see what you're doing from a high-level cost/benefit perspective. In addition to your periodic reports, invite senior management to your team meetings or for a walk around the shop floor. Show them what's changing and why.

> You must solicit and understand the needs of your audience.

- There's an art to "managing-up" with your boss. Understand what your boss wants and deliver it. In terms of communications, this generally means periodic updates (weekly) in the form of executive summaries for key activities—what's working and what isn't.

- Communicating with your peers is important, particularly since some portion of your initiatives will undoubtedly require cross-functional assistance. Give updates, keep people informed of the progress of key projects, and solicit feedback and suggestions to help instill a vested interest.

- Employees are the largest group that you'll be communicating with. In this regard, there are 5 "Cs" to consider as the fundamental underpinning to all of your communications efforts. Keep your communications **c**andid by always telling the truth; stay **c**ontextual by explaining to your team how the change agenda fits in the big picture of the organization; be **c**onstructive with your comments, working toward team unity; be **c**onsistent in all your messages; and provide **c**ontinuous communications reinforcing the change initiative.

- To the extent required, communicate with outside parties—that is, stockholders, distributors, suppliers, and customers—about the change agenda. Here, you want to sound confident about the undertaking, as well as appropriately reassuring about the progress being attained. Walk the fine line between treating these parties as true partners and protecting proprietary information and intellectual property. Seek help or input as needed.

Second, with all of today's sophisticated computer tools and offerings, you might think that we'd be pretty savvy in terms of exchanging messages across time and distance. Although electronics have significantly helped the logistical effort, they are hardly the most effective medium to communicate as, absent other communication cues, there is a fair amount of latitude for your message to be misinterpreted, interrupted, delayed, terminated, forwarded without your permission, or taken out of context. There are also those regrettable occasions when you wish you had never pushed "send" at all.

When choosing a communications medium, be sure that you match the proper conduit with the message you're trying to convey. For example, email isn't the forum to announce a facility closing or to prod people to work harder.

Weigh the salience of your message with how broad an audience you need to reach

> When choosing a communications medium, be sure that you match the proper conduit with the message you're trying to convey.

and how quickly. This will cause you to consider the most optimal communication channel available—which may cause you to move your lips instead of pushing a few buttons.

Third, repetition counts. For any single communications event or salient message, the tried and true adage of "telling them what you're going to tell them, tell them, and tell them what you told them" applies. This mindset keeps you on topic and increases the probability that your message is hitting home with your audience.

Last, keep your communications simple—tailored to the needs and interests of your audience. This doesn't mean dumbing down your message; rather, it means understanding and delivering what your audience needs to hear.

TRUTH

21

People can't drink from a fire hose

In our quest to be proficient communicators, we dictate correspondence, write reports, host nonstop meetings, leave after-hours voice mails—all with the good intention of directing and supporting our team.

The trouble is that your team may not appreciate—and may even resent—your efforts. For as much as communication is one of the key drivers toward the optimization of organizational performance, managers need to be aware of the potential downside of information overload.

People have a limited communication-processing capability. Continually interrupting, inundating, and overwhelming employees with information will cause one of two reactions. They will either multitask in an effort to keep up, or they will modify their work standards with various coping strategies.

> Managers need to be aware of the potential downside of information overload.

Either way, too much is too bad.

When people multitask, they're trying to do two or three things at once. When driving, it's the guy with one hand on the wheel and the other on his electric razor. At home, it's the parent watching television while helping with his child's school project. At work, it's your colleague who brings her mail and memos to a meeting or is responding to text messages while on the phone.

While you might think all of this juggling enhances productivity (85 percent of us do it, and 67 percent of us think we do it well), the opposite has been found to be true. A recent study found that the average worker lost ten IQ points while trying to simultaneously perform tasks. There is also a cognitive cost in the time and energy it takes to resume the original task that was interrupted, as well as the loss of mental downtime that allows our brain to store and organize our memories. Stress is also part of the equation.

Think about this the next time you want to roll out the messages associated with Six Sigma, process re-engineering, "pay for performance," quality circles, self-directed work teams, and the establishment of a learning organization. Inadvertently, you may be diffusing the energy that makes change happen—making your team more vulnerable, not stronger.

The alternative to multitasking involves embracing a personal coping strategy for information overload. Here, employees, at or beyond their capacity to process information, express their discontent and frustration—aimed at you for what they deem to be your irrelevance or irresponsibility—in a variety of ways. None are productive for them as well as the organization. Some minimal-effort strategies include ignoring the overload without making changes; "working to standards," essentially by working no more or less than required; and allowing unproductive queues to form around priorities. Related activities also include only attending to prioritized work, allowing clients to self-serve, and reducing performance standards.

The results of these strategies are declining output, decreased productivity, poor judgment and decision making, and increased error rates.

In light of these factors, you need to keep organizational communication efforts, particularly those that pertain to changing strategy and tactics, as simple, focused, and digestible as possible. Coordination and priority-setting are a must.

Your best barometer for measuring the quality and quantity of your communications is the direct feedback from your team members. Listen to their words, watch their behaviors for signs of overload, and test for understanding. In the ideal world, if you've effectively communicated your message, the kid in the mailroom with one stamp at the end of the day will know to put it on the customer correspondence as opposed to the magazine subscription renewal notice. And he will feel good about it!

> Keep organizational communication efforts, particularly those that pertain to changing strategy and tactics, as simple, focused, and digestible as possible.

TRUTH

22

Conversion is for missionaries and crusaders

Your natural inclination as a leader is to get everyone on the same page as quickly as possible—and rightfully so. Research tells us that engaged followers will generally experience greater job satisfaction, motivation, commitment, loyalty, camaraderie, clarity about values, pride and—most importantly from a business perspective—productivity.

You should be applauded for your intention; however, pragmatically, you might be wasting your time.

When faced with change, people tend to fall into one of three attitudinal camps, with what seems to be an almost bell curve distribution: The engaged folks are your can-doers, followed by your fence-sitters, and the naysayers.

The challenge for management is to identify whose level of commitment and engagement falls where, as quickly as possible, and to determine when and with whom staffing adjustments must be made.

Can-doers

The can-doers are your high performers who are supportive of and committed to the change mandate. They work hard; they work smart. They're self-motivated and results-oriented, have the highest standards of performance, embrace continuous improvement, and encourage and prompt others.

They will stay on the roller coaster for all its ups and downs, chins held high along the way.

You can't have enough of the can-doers on your team.

> The challenge for management is to identify whose level of commitment and engagement falls where.

Fence-sitters

Fence-sitters take up the majority of your parking spots.

Fence-sitters are equal and fluctuating parts enthusiast and skeptic. In many respects, they tend to be longer in service and, therefore, somewhat influential in opinion. They have "been there, done that." They fluctuate between ambivalence and negativity in reaction to change, until they can sort out whether it will threaten their personal organizational standing. They've seen it all and have relatively thick skins. They can also be most troublesome to identify, as they can have passive/aggressive tendencies and may speak through others in a nonattributable way.

From a managerial perspective, they need to be converted or pushed toward the can-doer population—one at a time—or towed away accordingly.

Naysayers

There's no cure for cynicism.

To your advantage, for the most part, these folks are the most readily identifiable.

In some cases, it's just not going to work. Reasons for nonparticipation will include nonperformance, lack of skills, values inconsistency, or those possessing an attitude or behavior that isn't conforming to the new norms.

Evidence for nonparticipation will consist of missed commitments, laziness and complacency, playing politics, risk aversion, deceit, apathy, absenteeism, withdrawal, rebellion, or retrenchment.

Although it sounds somewhat coldhearted, people demonstrating these behaviors and attitudes don't warrant your attention. Their costs are hidden in unrealized productivity, functional inefficiency, selfish priorities, poor customer responsiveness or relations, and potentially contagious poor morale. Their expense is real and significant in downtime, interim and replacement training, business interruptions, and the costs of recruiting a new hire.

While the management of many organizations rightfully believes that everyone deserves to be given an opportunity to meet new or different expectations, you should act with haste to remove these individuals from your team if they can't achieve the desired adaptive measures. In doing so, make these difficult decisions with appropriate haste wearing your business hat; execute the decision with fairness, respect for the individual, and compassion. The remaining employees will likely recover their own enthusiasm and commitment that much faster.

> Act with haste to remove these individuals from your team if they can't achieve the desired adaptive measures.

TRUTH

23

Organizational structure:
Look in from the outside

Whether it's one person with a Rolodex or a group of entrepreneurs in a garage, organizations in their infancy tend to be "open" environments—free of formal policy and procedure, with process-mapping and decision making being drafted on the back of an envelope.

Then, a funny thing happens. As an organization grows, its needs change. Before you know it, formal discussions are taking place about employee manuals, job levels, who can sign for what, and who gets what office furniture.

Of most importance for an expanding organization or one facing "better, faster, and cheaper" challenges are the choices to be made about the formal structure of the organization.

The structure of an organization is a derivative of economic and operational synergy—aligning the organization's vision; product; and operating, technological, and delivery capabilities with its primary stakeholders. Strategically, organizations—especially larger ones, are generally segmented, in whole or part, by function, product or service, matrix (a combination of functional and product or service), geography, outsourced resources, shared services, and project teams (teams dedicated to specific needs and deployed on a short-term basis as needed).

Decisions involving structure are important. Absent related discipline and protocol, the organization will suffer from ineffectiveness and inefficiencies. Unforeseen impediments, obstacles, bureaucracies, egos, "groupthink," or other restrictions will smother creativity, productivity, and enthusiasm.

Recognizing that there is no "cookie cutter" template for all organizations—given their unique natures and cultures, how then do you determine the ideal structure? The answer is fourfold:

1. **Involve the right people—those closest to the work at all levels—**This is critical, for it gives all participants the chance to put their personal stamp on the operation. This will, by extension, play an important role in changing the organization's culture and operating environment, and it will enhance the probability for the success of implementation.

2. **Contrary to the most common approach taken to address business challenges, you should start with a "blank slate" and look at the organizational structure from the "outside in," with the mindset of becoming your toughest competitor**—This requires an analysis of key strategic relationships; lines of business; common functions; shared services; customer responsiveness; and local/national/regional/global business requirements—with an outsider's objective perspective.

One of the world's largest appliance manufacturers recognized that its overall operating structure was a major contributor to its increasing red ink. In response, the CEO formed an internal six-person committee, comprised of a cross section of international and functional expertise, and

> You should start with a "blank slate" and look at the organizational structure from the "outside in."

charged them with researching, analyzing, and recommending a new blueprint for the way the company would operate and approach the market. This was a complex and demanding task as this company had more than 100,000 employees with operations in over 50 countries and more than 500 product lines.

For the better part of the next six months, the committee urgently gathered relevant information from two sources. Internally, they visited various facilities all over the world to gain sharper insight about the company's assets and limitations. In parallel, and with far greater emphasis and attention, they were also globetrotting to the headquarters of several other Fortune 100 companies to study their organizational structures and the rationale for each—attempting to synthesize "best practices," as well as their potential competitive application. They were also speaking to customers of all sizes.

Ultimately, the committee's "outside in" findings led to a corporate-wide organizational restructuring, focusing upon breaking up the "silos" of divisions, groups, regions, and countries. Operational and reporting changes included the consolidation of global product lines, leveraging the operational and distribution synergies, the formation of strategic partnerships, the outsourcing of competencies that were not considered as "core," the elimination of redundancy, expanded spans of control, and centralization and sharing of common resources and services. First-year financial savings were in the hundreds of millions of dollars.

3. **You need to have some concurrent debate and reach consensus about the characteristics of the new organization**—Words like *nimble, streamlined, flat, product/market/customer driven*, and *entrepreneurial* will likely be bantered about. This discussion will also determine where the appropriate level is to assign authority and accountability. Specifically, how willing are you to share decision making, leadership, project planning, conflict management, and rewards?

   The answers to these questions ultimately reflect how empowerment is practiced in your organization. Generally speaking, research has shown that empowered organizations tend to have fewer management layers with broad spans of control and local profit and loss responsibility; they have a small, facilitative head office with shared power and risk-taking; and they have a process-based structure that inhibits silos and functional kingdoms.

4. **Remember that you have a variety of subsequent staffing options available to you**—These include populating and supporting your organization with some combination of full-time employees, part-time employees, retained opinion leaders, on-demand consultants, contractors, and professional services providers.

Chances are that that you'll staff your team with full-time employees to handle the valley of workload and rely on contingency resources for the peaks.

In sum, change presents a wonderful opportunity to look at your organizational structure. Whether you're starting from scratch or you're a participant in a long-standing hierarchy, you should consider and identify a framework that ensures the maximum probability for the execution and attainment of your vision. Get lots of adhesive tape and index cards, and be creative. You will likely generate organizational pride, a collaborative spirit, and open minds.

24

Build your team around your "A" players

With the many balls you're trying to juggle about vision, processes, budgets, communications, and goal-setting, you may be inclined to put the "people issues" on the back burner for a while.

This is a recipe for trouble.

You only have two types of resources available: time and people. You can't afford to let one slip at the expense of the other. In fact, while it may sound counterintuitive, the former actually plays a secondary role to talent in the pursuit of new competitive space.

If you believe that people are your most valuable resource (as you should), then having the right person in the right place at the right time—preferably an "A" player—is essential for your success.

To do this, you must assess your team against your current and anticipated business needs.

You've likely inherited a team that has a variety of talent and attitudes. Some are stellar performers; some aren't. Some are ambitious; some are complacent. One or more may be disappointed that they don't have your job.

> Having the right person in the right place at the right time—preferably an "A" player—is essential for your success.

To assess your team within a reasonable period (90 days), you should get background information by speaking to other managers with knowledge of your team. Speak to your boss. Go through the personnel files looking at past performance reviews, academic credentials, and training records. When it's time to take pen to paper, you must formally determine the criteria to use to evaluate your talent. In this regard, consider the following framework—giving weight to each factor based on the situation and your personal preferences:

- **Competence**—Does this person currently have the technical competence and experience required to execute the responsibilities of the position?

- **Judgment**—Does this person exercise good judgment, particularly under pressure?

- **Energy**—Is this person energetic and enthusiastic?
- **Focus**—Does this person understand and stick to priorities versus meandering?
- **Relationships**—Does this person get along with others, is she team-oriented, and is she capable of conflict resolution?
- **Trust**—Does this person do as she says?

Be sure to meet with each team member as part of this assessment. Here, you need to probe their reflections and reactions to the organization's vision, strategy, and values. Get their thoughts about the present and future state of the business in terms of challenges and opportunities. Ask what they would do if they were "king for a day."

When you've completed your assessment, categorize each person as an "A," "B," or "C" player and contemplate her placement into the new organizational structure as if she had to reapply for her job.

> Ask what they would do if they were "king for a day."

"A" players significantly impact current and future growth. They add higher value to the organization based on skill set, knowledge, and role. They're highly intelligent, quick studies. They're adaptive, energetic, and possess a results orientation. They're the top performers—with even higher potential—and are most critical to the organization's long-term success. These are also the individuals who are most difficult to replace.

"B" players add high value, are solid performers, and are good corporate soldiers. They will compose the majority of your organizational population.

"C" players add marginal contribution.

Covet your "A" players. Build your organization around them. Place them in the first "slots" of your new organization structure, into positions of power and influence. Assign them to the greatest opportunities and challenges for your organization. Make sure they're retained to help lead, guide, and direct the organization's transformation.

"B" players are your backbone. You can leave them in their current assignment. You can consider them for future development and expanded responsibilities. Also, you can move them into another position that further leverages their strengths. In addition, you can defer any decisions about them until you have more information.

Shift "C" players to another position that better suits their skills, give them training or remedial opportunities, or replace them.

Where critical staffing voids exist, you must turn to the outside.

TRUTH

25

Candidate screening:
Let the facts speak for
themselves

In a scene from the movie *Miracle on Ice*, Herb Brooks, future gold-medal winning coach of the U.S. Olympic hockey team oversees the squad's tryouts when he tells his bosses—much to their political displeasure—he wants a team with the 25 best players; not the best 25 players.

Mr. Brooks's points of emphasis are worth considering, as there is a dramatic distinction in his words beyond semantics.

At some point, you will need to attract and select talent—the right talent—from outside your organization. This may sound like a daunting task—often involving job fairs, recruiting advertisements, multiple job specification reviews, and interviews—however, it need not be.

There is a little-known way to help you expedite the process. Let the candidates "self-select" by offering candid insight that allows them to realistically determine whether they want to work for you.

> Let the candidates "self-select" by offering candid insight that allows them to realistically determine whether they want to work for you.

In this regard, there are six key areas of organizational fit to discuss and probe:

- **Give a thorough overview of your company's culture, explaining its salient attributes and their day-to-day influence**—Not every workplace is right for everyone. Wall Street institutions, Pepsi, General Electric, hospitals, small law firms, and the post office each have unique expectations regarding personal performance and commitment—as does your organization.

Related to this, ask why the candidate is looking for a job (as well as the reasons for past job changes), trying to determine if he's running from his current organization as opposed to expressing a passionate view as to why he belongs in your organization.

- **Discuss your company's values, how they're embraced and manifested, and whether they're in alignment with those of the candidate**—In this regard, there are several often-enlightening questions that provide such insight. These include, "How would you define personal fulfillment?" "Tell me about a time at work where you had to bend the rules?" or "Have you ever compromised quality for speed?" Also, watch the detail of how a person interacts with others if you're meeting him outside the office.

  Individuals sharing your organization's values will most likely be your believers, cheerleaders, and articulate advocates. You should not invest in anyone if his personal values are not in alignment with those of your organization.

- **Determine if the candidate has relevant and applicable experience**—This is where you describe the position's near-term challenges, while determining if the candidate is at the appropriate level of professional growth (that is, early or more mature in his learning, an established practitioner, a functional expert, or an opinion leader) to make the desired impact.

- **Inquire about the candidate's job competencies using a technique called *behavioral-based interviewing***—This methodology provides insight into "what" an individual accomplished, as well as "how" (that is, with influence, knowledge, charisma, technical proficiency, leadership, and so on). It's predicated upon past behaviors and attitudes being repeated when confronted with a similar set of problems.

  Behavioral-based interviewing is particularly effective if there are multiple interviewers and there is advanced planning and coordination around who will ask what. You can find examples of behavioral-based interview questions in Appendix F, "Behavioral Interviewing Examples," on the book's web site.

- **Look for team players**—In your quest for "better, faster, and cheaper," you will place a premium upon individuals with proven employment records comparable to your current challenge to aggressively jump-start your organizational initiatives. Sometimes, the most talented individuals are the least likely to embrace a team approach.

- **Don't be afraid to hire people who are better than you**—David Ogilvy, the advertising genius known for building brands such as Rolls Royce and Hathaway, noted the secrets of success as, "First make a reputation for being a creative genius. Second, surround yourself with partners who are better than you are. Third, leave them to get on with it."

His second point is worth reflection here. You want people on your team with the highest level of mental ability. Assess the candidate's expertise, and make it clear that you not only expect to learn from him, but you also expect him to share.

Probing these key areas can help candidates determine their respective levels of comfort and interest about your organization—that is, self-selecting—while minimizing your probability of making a less than desirable hire.

TRUTH

26

Avoid the ten potential "placement pitfalls"

You may be tempted to take a few staffing "shortcuts" when it comes to external hiring or the reassignment of incumbents. The problem is that haste will likely cause more troubles in the long run.

In this regard, you must be cognizant of and avoid the following precarious mindsets or practices:

- **You think a Band-Aid will stop the bleeding**—While the short-term needs of any business can be pressing, try not to act in a "quick fix" manner that detracts from the organization's long-term horizon, particularly if there is a high probability of negative impact to an otherwise healthy workplace climate.

- **You believe everything on the candidate's resume**—It has been estimated that up to 40 percent of resumes have everything from little white lies and exaggerations to blatant misrepresentation.

  Resumes aren't fact sheets; they're "eye candy" with all the right buzzwords. They're designed to do one thing and one thing only—catch the attention of the hiring manager.

  If the paperwork looks too good to be true, it probably is. Bogus degrees, falsified credentials, lapses in employment, and other significant inflations and omissions are becoming more the rule than the exception.

  In response, try to obtain as much recent, reliable, and valid objective information as possible about the candidate by utilizing effective pre-employment screening and, to the extent possible, "back-door" reference checking procedures. For the latter consideration, always get information from prior supervisors, and document your conversations.

  > Try to obtain as much recent, reliable, and valid objective information as possible about the candidate.

- **You believe that every position must be filled with an "A" player or someone with leadership potential**—While it's true that you'll likely return faster and more often to an automotive service station staffed with more "A" players than its competitor down the road, it's not an absolute. You also need your share of good corporate soldiers.

■ **You put less than your best foot forward**—There is no upside to a lengthy employment negotiation. Act in good faith. Show all candidates and internal placements that they're "wanted" from the onset. Extend market-based employment offers that also consider internal equity, economic trends, the company's competitiveness, and succession planning, in conjunction with the candidate's employment history and expectations.

■ **You treat everyone the same**—To the contrary, fresh and innovative recruiting practices should be considered to accommodate the needs of today's workforce. In this regard, offering such benefits as flexible and part-time schedules and work-from-home allowances may be positively received.

■ **You try to fit a square peg into a round hole**—There once was a highly regarded professional with twenty-five years of industrial experience whose record of accomplishment as an individual contributor was the envy of his peers.

Then, as a result of some unexpected turnover, his manager asked if he would be willing to assume some supervisory responsibilities on an "interim" basis. That's when the trouble began—absent any formal guidance, training, or mentoring, he quickly alienated those he was relying on for critical input.

As it turned out, due to financial restrictions, nothing was interim about this assignment. The damage turned out to be long lasting. The individual derailed, and by consequence, his department failed at a critical juncture.

When faced with the original staffing dilemma, the management of his organization reacted poorly. They did not realize that the best individual contributor does not necessarily make the best manager.

The best individual contributor does not necessarily make the best manager.

■ **You fail to keep parties of interest informed**—Reduced ambiguity in the staffing process is something to be diligent about. Accordingly, after the interviews are completed, you (or your designees such as the recruiter or human resources representative) should collect and compile the thoughts from and reactions of each interviewer. This is an ideal time to identify any discrepancies that the candidate may have presented. It also serves as an opportunity to reinforce with all parties the competencies being sought.

■ **You aren't prepared for the water cooler**—As internal candidates are placed elsewhere in the organization, you should openly share the reason(s) for the move with colleagues.

For external hires, be prepared for any comparisons to current talent.

■ **You keep waiting for the "ideal" candidate**—This is a lot like waiting for Godot; it just isn't going to happen. In most cases, there will be some compromises or trade-offs between your job specification and each candidate's resume. Don't waste time or money "holding out" when you have someone who checks nine of the ten boxes.

■ **You think that you can change an individual**—The Oakland Raiders of the National Football League used to draft the best available talent and mold him to their system. It worked for a while, but several recent poor seasons have invalidated this theory.

To the extent possible, get people on your team, on day one, who share your business philosophy. Changing times may not afford you the luxury of time to convert others.

TRUTH

27

Don't surround yourself
with yourself

In our personal lives, a look around shows that we generally tend to surround ourselves with people of like interests and perspectives.

This paradigm doesn't work at a changing workplace.

As the world seemingly shrinks, with markets and products extending their global reach, it's becoming more the rule than the exception for managers to have teams composed of men and women with a range of multinational educational, ethical, business, and life experiences. In fact, many of us work in larger organizations or ones that may be contractors or suppliers to the U.S. government that are legally required to be in compliance with affirmative action guidelines that encourage this "mix."

Unfortunately, some managers confuse the terms *affirmative action* and *workforce diversity*, and while they're conceptually related, you shouldn't use them interchangeably.

Affirmative action is about comparing your workforce to the local population in terms of its representation of various factors such as gender and ethnicity. Its goal is to have your workforce appear as a statistical mirror and for you to explain and justify where and why it isn't. Its primary tool is a calculator.

Diversity is about mutual human understanding, appreciation of differences, and the extension of empathy. It's about inclusion, not exclusion. It's about the way we treat each other and interact. It's based on respect and dignity, not numbers. It welcomes fresh perspectives, and it encourages and empowers all employees to actively contribute to the overall success of the organization. Its primary tool is an open mind.

While some may view affirmative action as a chore, diversity should be embraced as an organizational imperative. To do so, you must seek out and blend the passions, commitments, and hearts and minds of each of your team members—cultivating and creating collective inspiration.

This is easier said than done.

> Diversity is about mutual human understanding, appreciation of differences, and the extension of empathy.

Many organizations fail to take diversity seriously as a business challenge—offering merely lip service or a passive day's training to the topic when it's a real, embedded, and ongoing problem to be managed at all levels. Not only is it the right thing to do, but also evidence shows that it's a key for competitive advantage.

First, diversity enhances team performance. This was validated in a study that found medical scientists performed especially well when they maintained ongoing work relationships with colleagues having a wide assortment of values, experiences, and disciplines. In fact, this study found that constant close association with colleagues similar to themselves decreased their performance.

Second, diversity leads to better problem-solving and decision making. This was reported in a study when mixed-gender groups consistently produced better-quality solutions than did all-male groups. The statistically significant findings included the fact that no all-male group ever scored higher than a mixed-gender group. Similarly, another study noted that ethnically diverse groups were more efficient, over time, in identifying problems and generating possible solutions.

Third, diversity is better for your bottom line. This was concluded in a study conducted by Cedric Herring, Ph.D., professor at the University of Illinois at Chicago. He found that "Racial diversity in a company's workforce leads to improved business performance." Specifically, Herring noted that, "Businesses with greater diversity reported higher sales revenues, more customers, larger market shares, and greater relative profits compared to firms with a more homogeneous makeup."

> Diversity leads to better problem-solving and decision making.

We are all travelers on a common organizational and life path. Seek out and welcome diverse perspectives and backgrounds, be cognizant of individual perspectives and grounding, and leverage the strengths and differences of each person so that balance and synergy might be achieved. After all, if the Scarecrow, Tin Man, Lion, and Dorothy— folks with diverse demographics and interests who bonded around a common cause and overcame numerous obstacles on the yellow brick road—could come together as a team, why can't you?

TRUTH

28

Why you need to get staffing right

Research indicates that up to six in ten executives fail to achieve desired results within the first 12 to 18 months of joining a new organization!

What could cause such a seemingly low batting average? After all, these leaders had the chance to "kick the tires" before coming on board—starting with a "clean slate," without political motives or baggage.

Part of the answer is found in acclimation—or more specifically, the lack of it.

After spending countless hours and significant resources to attract and select the brightest and the best talent and placing the individual into a dynamic environment with some risk, many managers fall into the trap of leaving it up to them to "figure it out." Initial ambiguity or a lack of specific direction is part of "on-the-job training."

This "hands-off" approach is fraught with peril. You must proactively ensure a "soft landing" for all newcomers, thus maximizing the probability for their integration, engagement, and retention.

Integration for a new hire or new team member may be achieved by becoming personally involved with the oversight and delivery of an individualized "on-boarding" process. This should include key staff and customer introductions, role delineation and communication, a review of functional accountabilities, intranet familiarization, a translation of the organization's alphabet soup (acronyms), participation in team-building forums, and a review of all policies and procedures. Also, if the new hire is relocating, you should provide resources to allow the individual to understand and appreciate local business customs and ethics, as well as business communication and interaction guidelines and protocols.

Engagement provides the individual with the linkage to meaningful work and personal fulfillment. In this regard, it isn't so much what you do, but how you do it—by utilizing a participative approach. To the extent possible and desirable by the employee, identify performance objectives and professional development goals within 30 days of hire. It's also your responsibility to provide a support toward these ends by ensuring that the employee has the proper tools, information, and resources, in a supportive work environment.

Retention is a critical early concern because the new hire is still vulnerable to the marketplace. She may still be in touch with her former employer. Retention has three related aspects:

■ **The cost of turnover is poison to your bottom line**—Intangibles such as lower morale, possible interruptions in key customer or supplier relationships, the loss of "tribal knowledge," and process inefficiencies are real. Tangible costs such as possible separation expenses (severance and possible litigation), recruiting fees, temporary help or consulting assistance, temporary training, internal reassignments, or increased workload and overtime for others to cover the gap can add up in a hurry.

At the executive level, estimates regarding the actual cost of replacement vary from a relatively conservative 5 times base salary to an astonishing 28 times! More conservative numbers hold true for the middle management and technical levels.

■ **Your new hire is a direct reflection on you**—By extension, his every action, word, decision, and interaction represents to the organization, in the most demonstrative manner, your actions, words, decisions, and interactions. Therefore, with your reputation on the line, you have a vested interest in making sure that your new hire gets off to the best possible start through his accelerated understanding of and adherence to your cultural norms and organizational values.

■ **The likelihood of your team gaining traction against the challenging objectives that you have identified is greatly increased when you have relative stability on your team**— Said differently, it's hard to win games when you're constantly short of players.

Managers who embrace a hands-on approach to helping their new hires acclimate will likely have fewer problems when it comes to morale and turnover. You may even make a friend or two in the process.

TRUTH

29

If you must "right-size," do it the right way

> The term *right-size* has negative connotations—seen as corporate doublespeak.

The managerial actions associated with this exercise—namely informing one of your team members that her position has been eliminated—are the toughest and most distressing part of your job.

Perhaps this is why many managers reduce staff so poorly. They prefer to avoid related decisions and discussions until the last possible moment—hoping that someone else may have to deal with it, there might be a last-minute change in plans, or the matter may somehow otherwise "go away."

To help with this endeavor, there are some things to keep in mind.

Explore all alternatives

Reducing force is hard on everyone. It should be used only as a last resort—as it may be viewed as unfair, draining valuable energy and focus from the organization. It may also undermine trust in management, making morale's recovery a difficult challenge.

Is the problem too little profit or too many people—or both? To the extent that operational alternatives can be considered first, they should. And how about trimming waste in other areas? Money can surely be saved by reducing travel costs; pursuing discount purchasing options; renegotiating vendor contracts; eliminating consultants; and delaying capital expenses.

Before reducing force, consider every possible option. Perhaps training is part of the solution. Maybe technology can somehow help, or a shift in strategy can direct resources in a more meaningful and productive manner.

Your business needs should drive the selection process

As you consider your anticipated business needs, you must determine how many employees are required to perform the needed tasks and what skills they must possess. If you have excess capacity, you have no choice but to reallocate or dispel those resources.

In a union shop, seniority determines who stays and who goes. It's called a "layoff" in that people have recall rights.

A "reduction-in-force" is what takes place in most office environments. Recent performance evaluations and skills among workers with similar job functions are the focal points for decision making, not personalities and relationships. All employee actions are considered final.

When you think your list is in pretty good shape, be sure to have your human resources professional, corporate attorney, or outside counsel with employment law experience review all materials.

Be proactive with communications

Ambiguity or absence of communications can create a void in your organization that might be filled with rumor and hearsay.

Be honest. Tell people what's going on and why. The subject matter isn't pleasant, but it's best to have open discussions and to deal with it. Allow people to freely speak their minds to give the remaining employees a chance to pause, reflect, and move forward in unity.

Treat everyone in accordance with your organization's values

How people are treated as they leave is important. It not only impacts those affected, but it also has a ripple effect on the morale and productivity of the "survivors." For as much as you think it's business, it is indeed personal. Very personal.

As with all separation choices, decide with your head; enact with your heart. Treat everyone with respect; treat them the way you would want to be treated. Be sensitive to the feelings and perspectives of those leaving, as they may be surprised, angered, hurt, and disappointed. To the extent possible, extend severance, benefits continuance, and career counseling. If your organization can be more generous, do so. This is a time to show you care.

> Treat everyone with respect; treat them the way you would want to be treated.

Give appropriate notice

This is a fine line to walk. The angel on your right shoulder wants to give people as much notice as possible so that they can be forward-focused, understanding the reality of the situation, and planning accordingly.

The devil on your left shoulder fears too much notice might result in a productivity drop, declining morale, apathy, or even sabotage. In addition, people might prematurely bail on you if you have transitional needs.

The real determining consideration here isn't so much timing; it's trust.

To the extent practical and reasonable, you should let people know what may be or is on the horizon. Surprises will cause your team to mistrust you and to lose their respect for you—particularly when the "survivors" find out that you had awareness of the situation well in advance. Without your team's trust or respect, your workplace climate runs the risk of turning toxic—which could take years to correct.

Be done with it

There was a time, particularly in the early-nineties, when large companies found themselves reacting to disappointing quarterly financial results by having layoff after layoff. This repeated exercise, without strategic intent or linkage, destroyed management's credibility, vanquished employee loyalty, and had a detrimental impact upon those organization's effectiveness and efficiencies.

Cutting off the dog's tail an inch at a time only has a downside. To the extent possible—recognizing that there are no future guarantees—try to get the downsizing behind you as soon as possible.

Prepare for tomorrow

Maybe there is nothing you can do to avoid the downsizing that you're faced with today, but you can prepare for tomorrow

Staff cautiously and deliberately. Build your team around a core group of employees to handle the minimal work requirements. Cross-train your team as possible—giving you organizational depth while your team members expand their life skills. As the business grows, consider using contractors and consultants as staffing options. Also, flexible workers—part-timers, telecommuters, retirees, and stay-at-home parents—might be part of the solution.

These contingent staffing resources can require customized compensation arrangements, but they can give you the flexibility you need until you can commit to a "full-time employee."

TRUTH

30

One style does not fit all

Early management science suggested that there were two schools of thought when it came to style: Theory "X" and Theory "Y"—with little in between.

With Theory X, managers believe that most workers have an inherent dislike for work and will avoid it if they can. They also wish to avoid responsibility and have relatively little ambition. Therefore, most people must be coerced, controlled, directed, or threatened with punishment to get them to put forth adequate effort.

With Theory Y, people enjoy work as a natural extension of their being. They welcome learning and actively seek responsibility. They exhibit self-control and self-direction in their efforts to achieve organizational results. They exercise a high degree of imagination, ingenuity, and creativity. To be properly managed, these people require more of a "laissez-faire" approach.

Over time, it has become recognized that these theories represent endpoints of the style spectrum, and there are variations based on factors other than a leader's predispositions.

Today, research suggests that there are four distinct leadership styles, determined by situational considerations, as well as your assessment of your team members' psychological maturity (their self-confidence and ability and steadiness to accept the job) and their job maturity (their relevant skills and technical knowledge). These styles include telling, selling, participating, and delegating.

Unlike times of business "status quo" when you utilize any one of these styles on any given day, you utilize each of these four leadership styles in an almost linear manner when leading organizational change.

Telling

In your fight against time, the first leadership style you gravitate toward is telling. Like a commander at the combat front, you draw upon your experience to provide specific instructions and closely supervise performance. You're autocratic, fighting the clock. You identify and control what needs to be done, by whom, and by when. Your goal is to stop the hemorrhaging and shift the organization's course as soon

You utilize each of these four leadership styles in an almost linear manner.

as possible. You're also assuming the greatest professional risk for the results.

This is the most difficult style at a personal level. Undoubtedly, you have to play the bad guy and make unpopular decisions about products, services, or processes. It may be your word that closes manufacturing plants or service centers and causes job loss—potentially impacting employees who had little to do with placing the organization in its current state of vulnerability. This is personally painful. Lost sleep may be part of the process, and you will not win any popularity contests. Hopefully, this style isn't needed for long—for any situation and for fewer and fewer individuals.

Selling

When the direction of the organization becomes less ambiguous and some short-term results come to fruition, your style will require more *selling*. Here, you explain decisions and provide opportunities for clarification. Your intention is to persuade people to voluntarily act in a supportive manner toward the information you provide.

This style employs your skills of charisma, as well as tests your levels of energy and enthusiasm. Your selling will likely prove frustrating as you try to get everyone as motivated and committed to the cause in the timetable you desire—and not everyone will be buying.

Participating

As the organization stabilizes, you should embrace a *participative style*, where ideas are shared and you play the role of facilitator. At this point, you still control (and always will) the decisions regarding strategy and resources, but you listen to the people in the organization closest to the work, as well as your customers, to develop related business plans.

This style involves giving select employees—if not everyone—a voice and some influence with the vote. It also requires letting people embark down a path that has some risk, and allowing them to be wiser for the experience, without your intervention.

Delegating

You evolve into a *delegating* mode where you turn over responsibility for most day-to-day decisions and actions to the employees requiring the least amount of guidance, and with whom you have the greatest trust. With this style, you let your team decide the required processes, resources, structure, training, information system needs, and staffing levels, within the guidelines that you provide. You welcome their ideas and suggestions; you encourage their creativity and innovation. You want them to accept "ownership" and accountability for the development and execution of these plans.

In this latter stage, organizational change is clearly an underpinning of your culture, and you will spend more of your time with people, not budget summaries. It is personally most gratifying; however, you cannot let your guard down. With this style, you are also watching the horizon for changes in any key organizational, operational, or marketplace performance indicators that will cause you to manage people or the situation differently.

TRUTH
31

You can influence without authority

You have a nice office or cube; maybe there's a nearby window. You have a shiny nameplate. You have the "title" you always wanted—reflective of progressive managerial accountability and good organizational standing. You proudly display your business cards in a holder on your desk. If anyone expresses doubts or questions about who's in charge, simply refer them to the organizational chart. Hollywood might portray you with charisma, confidence, and gusto, as you oversee the operations for your team.

In a few words—you're the "Top Dog!"

But beneath this Norman Rockwell-like veneer is a far different and more complex reality.

You're growing increasingly frustrated with the time it takes to get things done. Bureaucratic red tape seems to be more and more a part of your day. Cross-functional decisions take long on choices that you deem to be pretty straightforward. Correspondence feedback lags from parties at all levels. You just don't seem to be getting as much changed with and through others as you'd hoped.

Part of the solution to this dilemma may lie in understanding how power works in your organization and applying your lessons learned. This is especially true in a dynamic business environment.

Power is the ultimate managerial aphrodisiac. It concerns your ability to bring influence and subsequent change to people, processes, and systems. Over 70 percent of managers possess a high "power orientation" compared with the general population; "successful" managers score even higher.

When it comes to power, your challenge is twofold. First, by observation and experience, identify and align yourself with the real decision makers in the organization and the people whom they take advice from. Second, beyond the formal authority of your

> Over 70 percent of managers possess a high "power orientation" compared with the general population; "successful" managers score even higher.

position, determine how power may be obtained and judiciously used as a tool of influence with others.

Regarding the latter challenge, you may glean power from a variety of nonexclusive sources, such as the following:

What you share and how often will be the basis for trust in many of your organizational relationships.

- **Information**—Information is the ultimate power asset, particularly when you're the sole message source, caretaker, or provider. What you share and how often will be the basis for trust in many of your organizational relationships. It will also have a direct impact on your team's performance. (That is, as discussed later in this book, more sharing equals greater collaboration, which translates to enhanced productivity.)

- **Expertise**—Knowledge isn't power; however, its application is. Technical knowledge is about how things work; social knowledge is about people.

  As a source of expertise on a given subject matter, your words carry enhanced credibility and authority.

- **Coercion and reward**—You have the ability to recognize all of your coworkers. With your team, you also have the ability to reward, and coerce and punish.

  Your ability to govern these allows you a certain degree of direct and indirect control over other's behavior:

- **Personality**—Possessing passion, confidence, and charisma— like John F. Kennedy or Ronald Reagan—can cause others to identify with and admire you.

- **Deference**—Age, experience, and organizational tenure may cause others to comply with your words and intentions.

- **Obligation**—If you do someone a favor or go beyond the call of duty now, that person will likely feel indebted to return the favor at a future point.

- **Association**—If you want to look skinny, hang out with fat people. If you want to get things done in an organization, find a way to connect with the "movers and the shakers."

To use your power effectively, know where it's derived from and exemplify it appropriately. For example, if you represent yourself as having a certain level of experience or expertise, but it's later discovered that you don't, you will have done yourself and the organization a regrettable disservice. Likewise, if you threaten an employee with discipline, but you aren't prepared to follow through on the ultimatum; your managerial credibility will be eroded.

TRUTH

32

You can't work the plan if you don't plan the work

Your overall happiness, satisfaction, and productivity should improve, as you get more familiar—and presumably comfortable—with your organization and colleagues, right?

Wrong. A study of over 1.2 million employees found that most were quite enthusiastic when they joined their new company, but morale sharply declined within six months and continued to downwardly spiral for years thereafter.

If you want change to get traction in your organization—at any level, you can't afford to let your new or retained team members be part of this statistical norm. This is where performance management plays a key role.

Performance management is the primary tool for strategy deployment. It's a strong force on an organization's culture. It reinforces the organization's values. It tells people at a detailed and personal level what matters. It galvanizes them to initial action and commits them to certain ongoing behaviors. Most importantly, it reveals how serious management is about achieving its business objectives—communicating to all employees and stakeholders that change and progress are required.

Your ability to plan and manage performance is absolutely critical for your organization's success.

At the beginning of the performance cycle, you should reach a clear understanding with each of your team members of the desired outcomes and developmental objectives that should be accomplished and how these targeted contributions are connected to and aligned with the organization's goals. Here are a few helpful guidelines:

- Effective managers know that an overwhelming majority of people—almost 9 out of 10, want to know how their work contributes to the bottom line.

  To the extent possible, have your team members participate in their respective objective setting, explaining how their

> Your ability to plan and manage performance is absolutely critical for your organization's success.

work product drives and supports team work, as well as how it contributes to the greater good.

■ Be clear in discussing and outlining expectations around things such as your tolerance for surprises, appropriate risk-taking, office politics, expected communications intervals, and the need to be among the "first to know" regarding key updates.

■ Variety is the spice of life. You should attempt to provide latitude that includes a variety of tasks, autonomy, an appropriate balance between building relationships with colleagues and working independently, and continuous learning. Keep job descriptions flexible and encourage cross-function cooperation and support.

■ Provide ownership. In most Walgreens stores, each employee "owns" one aisle and is responsible for customer service, orderly product presentation and tagging, and housekeeping. If it works at Walgreens (and other places), why can't it work in your workplace?

■ It has been said, "What gets measured, gets done." However, be careful what you ask for. Too many or the "wrong" metrics may take you off course.

Some rules of thumb include making sure that the data used to measure progress is objective, readily accessible, reliable, and has clarity of purpose. Be sure that it's well defined and calculation methods are understood, particularly when cross-functional dependencies exist.

■ Be SMART. When identifying or adjusting individual performance objectives, be sure they're

Specific	Objectives must focus on specific results rather than on general or vague outcomes.
Measurable	If an objective cannot be measured (quality, quantity, etc.), it cannot be effectively managed or achieved.
Achievable	The best objectives should be challenging and require some stretch, yet they should be achievable.
Relevant	Objectives must be aligned with and support the organizational strategy and functional tactics.
Time bound	There must be a predefined timeline associated with all objectives.

- Integrate values into your performance management system.
- Identify learning opportunities and developmental goals.

Unfortunately, many managers take individual development for granted—with a mindset that it will come naturally from on-the-job training or work experience. Worse yet, many managers do little to aid employees in their search for job enlargement or enrichment, as they view this responsibility to fall solely upon the shoulders of the employee.

> **Managers should foster an environment that encourages and allows for individual growth development.**

While employees should assume responsibility for their career management, managers should foster an environment that encourages and allows for individual growth development as mutual benefits may be so derived. And, while economics may not allow for across-the-board formal investment through ongoing training and education, special, if not exceptional, care and nurture should be provided to those who will ultimately bear the responsibility for identifying and executing the future charter of the organization.

See Appendix G, "Types of Organizational Learning," on the book's web site for some developmental areas that you may draw goals from.

TRUTH

33

There's no excuse for excuses

"We can't afford to lose him at this critical juncture."
"It's really not that serious of an offense."
"Do you know how long it will take us to find someone with comparable skills?"

We've all heard excuses like these from other managers who would prefer to rely upon time, chance, or the possibility of divine intervention, rather than confront an individual about a performance problem. In many cases, the senior management of the organization accepts the poor performer's rationale or apathetically turns the other way.

Not only is this approach inexcusable—as it will likely exacerbate what is already a difficult situation—but it also amounts to a blatant disregard of managerial responsibilities. Feedback is an obligation!

You will spend approximately 2,000 hours per year with the people you manage. Accordingly, in the interest of personal growth

Feedback is an obligation!

and personal development, all employees deserve objectivity and fairness in receiving timely feedback regarding the progress attained toward their individual goals, as well as how they embody the organization's values. This is especially critical in a dynamic work environment.

Providing performance feedback, especially when addressing a problem, can be a challenge. However, there are some best practices that will maximize the effectiveness of the process and minimize the likelihood that you'll have a serious employee relations issue on your hands.

Seek input—Prior to giving feedback, you should check with other employees, particularly managers who have direct observations to lend about the employee's performance, attitude, development, or ability to live by your organization's values.

Accurately diagnose the problem—Work performance depends on many variables. Try to determine if the failure to meet expectations is a result of values dissonance, aptitude, skills, a misunderstanding of the task, relationship matters, a lack of effort, or some outside influences.

Be honest—Feedback is a gift. A good feedback and coaching session is like a long look in the mirror; one needs to know what's working, as well as where some touch-up work is required. The best feedback helps people candidly see what they can't, allowing for candid guidance, assessment, and course validation and/or correction.

Be specific—From time to time, even the most well-intentioned employee does not understand or appreciate the consequences of her behavior, especially if her words and actions have a negative impact on other organizational participants.

Your feedback should be supported by factual data, including specific examples of observed performance and behavior. This will help employees understand and respond to the feedback.

> Your feedback should be supported by factual data, including specific examples of observed performance and behavior.

Meet frequently—You should hold regularly scheduled coaching and feedback meetings with your team members, which should be supplemented with ongoing or more frequent feedback on a less formal basis.

Intervene as required—If you were in charge of manufacturing and your widget-making machine suddenly started churning out defects, chances are that you would take immediate corrective action. This same sense of urgency should apply to people.

Don't procrastinate. And if the issue is of a sensitive or personal nature that may prompt a defensive response, practice or role play your delivery, frame your conversation around your desire to help, and remain stern in your conveyance of the need for corrective measures. While easier said than done, hopefully, your words will be received as constructive, developmental input.

Put it in writing—Recognize that feedback is a judgmental process. Writing down the specific results and details of work activities as they occur can help minimize subjectivity and the potential for misunderstanding.

Appraise the performance, not the person—During the Civil War in 1863, President Abraham Lincoln had the unenviable task of communicating some unflattering feedback to General Joseph Hooker, head of the Union Army at the Potomac. Specifically, the president needed to temper the rambunctious general, who was apparently placing his personal zeal and ambition ahead of the collective good of the army by placing far too many troops in harm's way.

In his seven-paragraph letter, Mr. Lincoln initially praised the general with heartfelt enthusiasm, referring to his bravery, skill, and confidence. The president then raised his concerns, suggesting that he was "not quite satisfied" with the general's strategy and aggressiveness as it impacted the welfare of the soldiers, leaving open the door for the consideration of options. The letter concludes with the President encouraging the general to have heightened vigilance, while pledging his continued support.

In the content and spirit of this letter, Lincoln successfully utilized diplomacy, provided timely and constructive feedback about the situation, and made it clear a change was needed—while not demotivating his powerful field commander.

This is a perfect example of understanding the difference between feedback and personal criticism. The former objectively focuses upon the actions taken, their ramifications, and the need for corrective measures; the latter takes aim at the individual's personal attributes—generally in a caustic manner.

Obtain training—If you aren't experienced or require a refresher course in performance management and assessment, pursue training, as these critical activities ultimately determine your team's career planning, merit increases, promotions, and corrective measures.

TRUTH

34

Know what buttons to push

Perhaps a product of today's "extreme makeover" mentality, there are many managers who think that with the "right" coach, resources, effort, practice, tutoring, training, incentive, education, mentor, or magic wand, the behavior or attitude of most team members can be changed.

This view is right; it's also wrong.

Anecdotal evidence suggests that if you want to change an individual's behaviors or attitudes to a more desirable end—at any time and in any circumstance, you need to provide answers to two key motivational questions: "What's in it for me?" and "Why should I care?"

Of course, to get the answers to these questions for each member of your team, you might have to hire an industrial psychologist to spend some time with each of your team members. After all, what one person finds exciting, another might deem a bore. Where one can't contribute, another might lead the way.

> You need to provide answers to two key motivational questions: "What's in it for me?" and "Why should I care?"

You need not go to such trouble or expense.

In his book, *Motivational Management*, Alexander Hiam outlines an "incentive profile." In the form of a scaled survey, this profile asks employees to consider 15 different motivators. These include the following:

- **Affiliation**—Desire to feel part of the group you work with.
- **Self-expression**—Urge to express yourself through your work.
- **Achievement**—Drive to accomplish personal goals. Pursuit of excellence.
- **Security**—Need for stability or reduction of uncertainty and stress.
- **Career growth**—Urge to develop your career to its fullest.
- **Excitement**—Impulse to seek new experiences and enjoy life through your work.

- **Status**—Motivation to increase your standing through accomplishments.
- **Purpose**—Need for meaning and direction. Desire for important work that really matters.
- **Competition**—Competitive spirit. Desire to excel in relation to others.
- **Recognition**—Need for positive feedback and support from the group. Desire to be appropriately recognized for your contributions.
- **Consideration**—Preference for a friendly, supportive work environment.
- **Autonomy**—Need for more control over your working life.
- **Rewards**—Motivation to earn significant rewards or wealth from one's work.
- **Responsibility**—Motivation to play a responsible leadership role.
- **Personal needs**—Need to satisfy essential personal or family priorities.

Hiam suggests administering this survey to each of your team members (or at least having a related discussion) and using it as a basis for mutual understanding by reviewing the findings with each individual to their level of comfort, determining the few motivators that matter most, seeking their input, and trying to satisfy those needs by assigning work opportunities around them.

Most everyone wants to work in an environment where there is trust, good communications, the opportunity for contribution, emotional support, clear goals and feedback, and an esprit de corps. However, they also want to reap the fruits of their efforts. As a manager, to modify your team members' behavior and attitudes, as well as to further motivate them to higher levels of performance, you must understand and respond to each person's needs.

TRUTH

35

Calm waters make for easier sailing

You may think that once individual performance objectives have been identified, your employees should be off and running in terms of executing the change agenda and you can exhale.

This would be a mistake.

Despite best intentions and efforts, change management deliverables have a mixed report card against sought-after expectations. Research has found that only about half of joint ventures and only a third of big mergers—the ultimate organizational change—do work.

What causes such projections to go astray? The answer is usually found in your organization's culture.

An organization's "culture" is a mix of many different factors, such as observed behaviors, norms and rites that involve working groups, values embraced by the organization, and the managerial philosophy and attitudes of senior management. Its impact is all-encompassing as culture helps define, among other factors, an organization's patterns of communications, how problems are solved, who participates in decision-making, the language used, the physical environment, and policies and procedures.

An organization's culture can be a valuable indicator of loyalty and commitment. It is an intangible that requires your full time attention.

When you sense any uneasiness within your team's culture about the change agenda, it's time to quell the concerns.

An organization's culture can be a valuable indicator of loyalty and commitment.

First, human nature tends to fear and resist change. This is driven by the potential erosion of—through the possibility of a diminished paycheck or professional capacity— our needs for physiological satisfaction, safety and security, love and belonging, and recognition and status. Change also threatens our personal "cocoon of perceived indispensability," wherein we fool ourselves into believing that our role is too valuable to the organization—only to find out otherwise.

You must address this with firm and convincing optimism. Discuss the desirable state of the organization and how every role contributes toward this end. Present the challenge as an opportunity to learn new skills, abilities, and attitudes. Build employees' self-esteem through your expressed confidence in them. Explain the roadmap in small journeys, allowing for easier understanding and adaptation. Suggest that change is in their self-interests for their professional self-preservation, development, and perpetuation.

Second, complacency could be a prevailing mindset within the organization that leads people to be too comfortable and reliant upon the business models that have resulted in their past success.

Complacency is best combated with information, but you need to be cognizant of both the medium and the message you desire to convey. Give as much relevant information and as many facts as possible. Probe employees' understanding with reflexive questions. Compel them to action by pointing to examples of what may happen if new thinking and work practices aren't embraced.

When employees come to view change from a similar perspective, they will likely perceive similar causes and solutions for it.

> When employees come to view change from a similar perspective, they will likely perceive similar causes and solutions for it.

Third, values dissonance can hinder any ongoing change process. Value is both a verb and a noun. Values provide a framework for your culture. They should be introduced into your organization with kid gloves, not a hammer.

At an individual level, you should take every communications opportunity—especially where change is topical—to reinforce the organization's values. This will help drive the salience of this message in the most personalized manner.

Within your organization, values and ethics should be likewise reinforced and "institutionalized." For example, J&J has Credo workshops for executives; Sun Microsystems has a "business conduct office" and places all top executives and financial managers through its "Fiduciary Boot Camp"; business schools are expanding their curriculums to include courses upon values-based ethics and responsibility; most larger organizations have confidential "whistleblower" hotlines; and all companies are responding to Sarbanes-Oxley about corporate/personal responsibility.

If workshops and class attendance are not viable options, you should, at a minimum, hold staff meetings that focus upon and periodically reinforce the organization's values.

You can find examples of how to address values at a collective level in Appendix H, "Prompting a Dialogue About Values," on the book's web site.

Fourth, one of the toughest challenges is to confront the individual considerations of inadequate skills and competencies, or the lack of performance. In these cases, you must reinforce the organization's vision, the need for organizational transformation, and subsequent individual change. In good faith, visibly demonstrate your commitment to help each person attain the needed skills through the provision of training and educational resources. To the extent possible, allow people who will be affected by the change to participate in deciding what needs to be done and how to implement the changes.

> Visibly demonstrate your commitment to help each person attain the needed skills through the provision of training and educational resources.

Last, there may a trust issue. Look in the mirror. Is there any way that your team might sense a lack of commitment or sponsorship? Have you been guilty of playing favorites? Do you have a personal insecurity that surfaces in ways that you aren't even aware?

The matter of trust is further explored in the next Truth.

TRUTH

36

Trust is a currency not easily earned, but easily spent

Former presidential candidate Gary Hart stated something to the effect of "Do as I say, not as I do." Charles Barkley, former professional basketball superstar, once claimed that he's "not a role model." In our Catholic churches, it's getting increasingly difficult to find an archdiocese not haunted by scandal.

In corporate America, despite or perhaps because of additional corporate governance, there has been a reported increase in the discovery and subsequent reporting of corner office misleading and misdoing. You need only to pick up the day's newspaper to read who is now in trouble, claiming innocence as the handcuffs are applied.

Unfortunately, we live in skeptical, if not pessimistic, times when it comes to personal accountability and trust.

The good news is that it need not be that way.

Trust is the glue that holds together all relationships. It makes organizations work. It's the most significant predictor of individuals' satisfaction with their organizations.

Trust is a character issue. You have direct control over it. If you want the trust of your team, you can't delegate responsibility for or claim ignorance of values or ethics. You must, by example and in all interactions, act and direct in a way that is consistent with the expected organizational values and norms for behavior, making the proper choices in ethical and moral matters. This is leadership personified.

There are only two ways to earn trust—having congruence between your words and your actions, and showing that you care.

As research indicates that most of us gain our understanding of the corporate world through upward observation, here are some tips to keep in mind as your team is watching you:

> There are only two ways to earn trust—having congruence between your words and your actions and showing that you care.

■ Lead by example.

■ Never ask someone to do something that you wouldn't do yourself; therefore, be sure to occasionally work or be in attendance for an off-shift or holiday.

■ Set an example with your presence. Arrive early; stay a little later. Get to meetings on time and be prepared. Return phone calls on the same business day. Address everyone in a manner reflective of a business setting. Dress appropriately.

■ If you work in a "staff" role, consider getting to occasional operations meetings, thereby enhancing your business knowledge, while keeping your team concurrently informed.

■ If you work in a large facility with a shop floor, consider a satellite office or desk closer to the operations, or at least dedicating part of your time to being accessible to the broader population. If your team is geographically diverse, try to get some time in the field.

■ Recognize that how and where you spend your time is important; pushing paper may endear you to a few, but not many. Face-to-face dialogue and exchange should be encouraged. Also, are you devoting your time on priorities or getting lost in the detail of lesser issues? Are you expressing concerns or being a church mouse?

■ Never let your guard down.

Reacting to a tragedy in which a groom-to-be was shot and killed by 51 bullets from the guns of New York City police officers in November 2006, Mayor Michael Bloomberg raised the observation that people should use restraint before rushing to judgment. In further commenting on the matter—in a seeming contradictory manner to his own advice—he also said that the number of shots seemed excessive.

He later clarified his "excessive" observation by stating that he was speaking not as a mayor, but as a private citizen.

In the eyes of all of his constituents, Mayor Bloomberg isn't and will never be a private citizen.

Whether you're at work, a social gathering, a service award dinner, or the company's holiday party, you're always a leader.

- Unless what you're told jeopardizes someone's safety or violates the law or a company policy, you must safeguard confidences at all times.

- Show your vulnerabilities. Your team can help you develop professionally.

- Carry a sense of humor. It's important, and it can be the needed organizational medicine. A manager should laugh first at himself or herself, and others thereafter.

- Admitting mistakes and learning from them is part of individual and collective growth and maturity. It also demonstrates confidence and humility, and it may be a platform for renewed team unity. JetBlue's CEO and founder, David Neeleman, is an example of this, taking the debacle of the 2007 Valentine's Day storm that snarled air traffic for days and turning it into an opportunity and pledge for better customer service going forward.

- Learn how to lose. You *will* mess up. Learn from the experience, recover, and apply the new knowledge. It will not be the end of your career. Pick up, brush off, and move forward.

- Set standards for productivity and quality, and then walk the talk. If you want people to model their behavior after you—and they will—you must practice what you preach.

- Take every opportunity to show that you care deeply about the well-being of every employee, as well as for the long-term interests of the organization.

One cautionary note: The fastest way to vanquish credibility and trust is to create a double standard around your words and actions. Some of the most violated examples of this organizational incongruity are in the cost-cutting area when exceptions are made to a hiring freeze or the elimination of consultants; a travel ban or the elimination of certain reimbursements; or new expense guidelines. It never seems to fail that the party making the exceptions is the one mandating the broader need for them.

TRUTH
37

If you're out of sight, you're probably out of touch

You need to manage change; don't let it manage you.

In the February 18, 2007 edition of *The Washington Post*, Dana Priest and Anne Hull wrote a story, "Soldiers Face Neglect, Frustration at Army's Top Medical Facility."

In this article, the writers described how the number of casualties from the war in Iraq has overwhelmed the Walter Reed Medical Center, to the point where the soldiers classified as outpatients are treated across the street in a facility called Building 18.

If overcrowding was the only issue, the journalists may never have taken to the keyboards; however, their investigation found far greater ills. Our rehabilitating veterans were enduring a facility that was in desperate need of repair—with problems including rot and mold, rodent infestation, and a dire lack of facility maintenance and planning. Further aggravating these shortcomings was a bureaucracy that seemed incapable of helping and often threw endless paperwork or apathy at those with the pronounced healing needs.

The story is a tragedy. But, it got worse.

In the days following the publication of the article, it was widely reported that this topic came as "news" to many senior governmental and military officials, including the Secretary of the Army, Dr. Francis J. Harvey. It appeared that his first knowledge of these deplorable conditions and the poor treatment given to our heroes came from reading the paper! Dr. Harvey later resigned.

There are some managerial lessons from these unfortunate events. It's your responsibility to keep a "pulse" on your team, fighting the temptation and natural tendency to be chained to your desk. In this regard, you must be visible and accessible; you need to "manage by wandering around" And it may surprise you to know that this practice is more effective than any other type of workplace climate survey or suggestion box program.

> You must be visible and accessible; you need to "manage by wandering around"

First, managing by walking around establishes rapport and builds goodwill. For example, Jerry Senion, the vice president of operations at a large manufacturing site for a Fortune 500 concern spent a portion of each day walking the factory floor, discussing the site's operations, finances, safety record, and the weather with those within earshot. He was constantly in motion, seeking out those who might otherwise be overlooked, as well as those who desired a platform. Jerry knew many of the site's 2,500 employees—viewing every individual as an important organizational asset and as the family's respective breadwinner. These walkabouts allowed him not only to deliver his messages, but they also created opportunities for personal connectivity, engagement, and collective learning.

Second, managing by walking around allows you to track the pace and efficiency of the change process, firsthand—without being seen as interference. There are no barriers, no filters. You can talk to the team and make your own assessment about what is and what isn't working. Your decision making will improve, as you will have more timely and accurate information.

Third, you will hear about and respond to the individual's or the team's day-to-day problems as they occur, preventing them from building into major issues. By inviting input, you demonstrate respect and establish trust. Your personal credibility will be enhanced if you respond to their respective needs.

Fourth, you will establish informal feedback loops about your performance. Ed Koch, New York City's former mayor, frequently asked his constituents, "How am I doing?" His style was a bit brash, but his question was indeed purposeful.

With such upside, managing by walking about is a tool for every manager.

Want to get started? Go slowly at first in terms of breaking the ice. You don't want to be seen as a threat. Remember, managing by walking about isn't a casual stroll through your facility; it has purpose and should be scripted. If necessary, take a notepad with you to take notes or prompt discussion points. This strategy is most effective if you demonstrate courtesy, give total attention to the persons you're speaking with, critically listen, encourage two-way dialogue, and show your appreciation for employees' candor.

And be sure to follow up as needed with any and all outstanding inquiries, even if they seem trivial to you.

38

Teams aren't a necessary evil

Teams are the backbone for getting things done in an organization. But there are pros and cons.

Think about the last poorly managed team that you were on. Members arrived late to meetings and were unprepared. Deadlines were never kept. Trust was never established; goals were not crisply identified and lacked consensus. People spoke more *about* each other than *to* each other.

Now remember the way that you felt. You may have resented the team leader for not taking more control. You may have been quietly or even visibly upset at your teammates for their seeming lack of respect. Your frustration grew and apathy increased. Taking your productivity clues from your peers (as research indicates), you adopted an "If they can get away with it, why can't I?" approach.

There is a significant managerial takeaway from this experience. If you allow bent rules, shoddy workmanship, and deadline exceptions for some team members, you can expect a line outside your door seeking the equivalent.

You can't allow this chaos.

When you organize ad hoc teams or subgroups with defined endpoints to take on a "change challenge," there are certain managerial competencies you can embrace and practice that will maximize the probability that people will remain true to the task at hand.

> There are certain managerial competencies you can embrace and practice that will maximize the probability that people will remain true to the task at hand.

Competencies are composed of skills, but they also include the underlying or "hidden" characteristics of an individual that drive behavior, such as values, self-image, traits, and motives. They involve understanding intentions, actions, and outcomes in job performances. They're learned, developed, refined, and practiced over a career—through role-playing, trial and error, developmental assignments, and coaching. They reflect how a person might behave, think, or be generally disposed.

In considering the must-have competencies for managing teams in the "better, faster, and cheaper" world, evidence says you need to possess or gain proficiency in the following.

- **Achievement orientation** emphasizes innovation and continuous improvement—performing more efficiently, more effectively, more competitively, and at a lower cost. At the personal level, this involves committing yourself to accomplishing challenging objectives or competing against a self-defined standard of excellence.

- **Directness** is using your personal power or the power of your position appropriately and effectively, with the long-term good of the organization in mind. This includes a theme or tone of "telling people what to do." The tone ranges from firm to demanding.

- **Teamwork and cooperation** are about your intention to work with others, to be part of a team, and to work together—as opposed to working separately or competitively. For this competency to be effective, your intention should be sincere.

- **Developing others** concerns your genuine intent to foster the learning of your team with an appropriate level of need analysis. Its focus is on the developmental intent and effect, rather than on a formal role of training.

- **Interpersonal understanding** promotes appreciating, interpreting, and responding to others' concerns, motives, feelings, and behaviors; and accurately recognizing strengths and limitations in others.

- **Team leadership** is when you express and act upon your purposeful desire to take your team to greater heights.

When you organize teams, clearly articulate their purpose and objective. Outline the timetable, context, and importance of their task. Set parameters for risk-taking. Discuss the resources available to the team and who the beneficiary will be from these efforts. Identify any boundaries that should be honored. Make the team members aware of their authority. Be clear in explaining your role as a visible sponsor, facilitator, and champion.

> When you organize teams, clearly articulate their purpose and objective.

151

Let the team members set their expectations for behavior, information flow and exchange, inclusion, leadership distribution, and the sharing of power. Be sure they know how and when to keep you informed.

From the team's onset through evolution, be cognizant of and practice these managerial competencies. You will likely find that you're on a path toward optimized performance.

TRUTH

39

Your way may not be the best way

There's nothing more tempting to one's managerial ego than a good old-fashioned Theory "X" edict, when you get to exert your power and authority on all those in your organizational kingdom. Yet, in all likelihood, your unilateral signal-calling only increases the probability that you're taking your team down the wrong path.

While it's easy to laugh at the joke that the camel is a horse designed by committee, research suggests that problem-solving, particularly involving complex and novel business challenges, is best addressed by a team of individuals with a variety of backgrounds, experiences, opinions, and knowledge.

In this regard, a good manager, when faced with significant operational challenges, must be more interested in finding solutions through others than in having her own way. This means inviting the thoughts and opinions from those closest to the work processes for the improvement of quality, throughput, and cost.

> Be more interested in finding solutions through others than in having your own way.

Such participation, although admittedly more time-consuming, instills a sense of ownership and accountability and will likely enhance productivity and unity around the course of action to be taken.

Of course, as a natural byproduct of this approach, there will also be some managerial challenges when these varied opinions bump into each other.

While a certain level of natural tension within a group or between two people is healthy, friction can be stressful and counterproductive. Don't let your uneasiness or your fear of being seen as too dominant interfere with your need to intervene. When conflict occurs, it's best to address it in a timely manner. Know your conflict-management style options, as well as an approach.

In terms of style, you must choose the one most appropriate to deal with the situation.

■ Cooperative problem solving enables people to work together toward win/win solutions. It aims for mutually beneficial and satisfying outcomes through collaboration.

■ Competing means that one party's interests will take priority over another's. It results in a win/lose outcome. It's most damaging to the relationship.

■ Compromising allows trade-offs. Each party sacrifices some of its intended outcome in the interest of moving forward; however, the solution may be suboptimal, and no one may like it.

■ Avoidance is an option, but it isn't generally recommended. Essentially, it says, "You decide and leave me out of it." It's akin to putting your head in the sand.

■ Accommodating means that you put your interests last, allowing the other party his way. You would choose this style if you value the relationship far more than the salience of the issue in dispute.

The "best" style allows for cooperation on a path toward mutual gains.

In terms of approach, there are seven steps of conflict resolution:

■ Decide when and where to intervene. Have your key points prepared. Anticipate responses.

■ Speak to the other person in a calm, polite, and professional manner.

■ Distinguish between positions and interests. People naturally tend to take positions about issues, especially when in a conflict. Underlying these positions are generally broader interests, such as security and the well-being of one's family. Interests usually relate to basic needs, while positions are opinions about how to achieve those needs. Positions may appear mutually exclusive, while interests tend to overlap.

■ Don't express hostility with your words or expressions. It's okay to disagree; it's not okay to be disagreeable.

■ Listen to understand. When you focus your full attention on someone with the intention of improving understanding rather than winning an argument, it helps create a relationship conducive to mutual problem solving.

- Express interest and empathy in what the other person is saying. Try to understand the other person's motives. Respect each other; face problems together. Help people shift their energies to focus on common concerns rather than seeing each other as the problem.
- Communicate clearly, offering positive suggestions. Be flexible as required.

Although we may not always have a choice about the conflicts we find ourselves in, it's possible to choose our response to them. Peace is generated by the moment-to-moment choices we make in dealing with conflict in our relationships within our organizational community.

TRUTH

40

The whole is greater than the sum of the parts

Not every manager in corporate America understands that teams have a better chance of being successful when they have integrated and understood roles toward a common goal, but you should.

There once was an executive who became so disgruntled from his work that he literally closed his office door throughout the workday. Ultimately, this individual separated from the company—at the company's request, within a few months of his hire date.

What could have possibly happened to so rapidly spur this individual's demise?

With the benefit of hindsight, the hiring manager apparently became so enamored with this individual's background and experience during the recruiting process that the position's job description was significantly expanded, particularly in terms of influence and authority. In doing so, the hiring manager was successful in wooing the recruit; however, she unfortunately failed to communicate these role modifications to others in the organization.

By consequence (and you can see where this is going), the new hire joined the organization with heightened expectations of his ability to contribute. His role then became the hub of an intense and competitive political wrestling match over turf issues that distracted and upset many of the senior players. This resulted in an inordinate amount of company-wide dysfunction. By the time any damage control efforts could intervene, the organizational and personal wounds were too deep for healing.

Research has shown that collaboration, not competitiveness, improves team performance. This is particularly challenging in today's business world when many of today's corporate teams are "virtual"—attempting to function without close proximity, while continually addressing responsibility and resource issues.

Competition results when people are working at cross-purposes. It focuses on a win/lose outcome. Someone will be subordinate to another. It precludes the effective use of resources. People feel

> Research has shown that collaboration, not competitiveness, improves team performance.

threatened and frustrated. They may relish in another's shortcomings or failure. They see others as an impediment to their selfish goals and interests. They may, intentionally or not, mislead or interfere with each other. There is no self-disclosure, as people fear being exploited. Hostility and low productivity are likely a result.

Collaboration is about superior productivity. People succeed when others succeed. They aid each other, in good faith, toward a common and understood goal. They're encouraging, and they understand each other's priorities. They can expect help and assistance from others, as it's in everyone's self interests. Intentions, feelings, and ideas are exchanged. Interactions result in cohesiveness and high morale. Team members also experience greater job satisfaction and commitment in this environment.

You also personally benefit from collaboration, in that your team will deem you to be more credible and influential.

How can you instill collaboration? The key is to make sure that the left hand knows what the right hand is doing, and they are working in unison. You do this through shared goals and shared roles.

Shared goals bind a team, and you need to make those goals (your vision and strategy) the underpinning of all activities. Encourage people to work in a cooperative manner. Help them recognize that everyone's contribution is equally important to the result. Like oarsmen on a ship, make sure that people understand that they have more to gain in working in unison. Align your processes and systems accordingly.

In terms of shared roles, openly discuss and communicate individual and collective accountabilities. One of the best ways to do this is to create and distribute a functional organizational chart that briefly lists each person's accountabilities in "bullets" under her name. This, or a similar exercise, generates corporate and functional transparency, furthers the understanding of the organization's critical path, identifies dependencies, allows for the appreciation for each other's efforts, and reduces individual silos and parochial interests.

With this collective understanding, organizational effectiveness and efficiency will be enhanced.

TRUTH

41

Embrace—don't run from— the questions

> There must be something in the human gene pool that causes most of us to avoid public speaking.

This philosophy plays out on both sides of the desk, conference table, or podium. The speaker may fear being asked a question, as he may dread the potential embarrassment associated with not having an answer. Likewise, audience members are self-conscious. They don't want to look silly or uniformed if they can't articulate or frame their inquiry in a manner that most will view to be constructive and educational.

You can eliminate all of this trepidation with a few managerial pointers.

You must establish a "safe to say" environment

"Safe to say" is an environment created by the way in which you interact with people. It allows participants to constructively express themselves without giving thought to politics, retribution, or other sensitivities. (The Japanese have a wonderful word, "honne," to describe this practice as speaking from the heart.) It's a place, perhaps utopian—but worth striving toward—where team members may put aside their inhibitions in order to openly and honestly share their thoughts and feelings. Communication should be free flowing, participatory, and without hesitation. This holds true for the good news and bad, in a setting where all input and feedback is accepted; where facts, fiction, and all the rumors may be discussed.

> "Safe to say" is an environment created by the way in which you interact with people.

You should lead with questions

There are bound to be a lot of questions, particularly during times of organizational change. You can encourage their asking, but you should also ask a few of your own, encouraging discussion and debate.

The best questions are open-ended. They require thought beyond a simple "yes" or "no." These allow participants to come up with their own answers—creating opportunities for collective learning, as well as the establishment of some basic rapport. In a nonjudgmental manner, they bring optimism, show thoughtfulness, build community, and provide clarity on the path toward solution.

Examples of open-ended questions include: "Tell me why you feel this way?" "Can you further explain this to me?" or "What are our possible options?"

Related to this point, you must avoid being judgmental by steering away from asking any questions that might evoke a defensive response such as, "Who is to blame?" "What's wrong with them?" and "Why bother?"

You should be a critical listener

Did you ever notice that you need the same letters to spell the words "listen" and "silent"? Critical listening helps others explore all sides of an issue; often restating the issue, thus demonstrating your understanding of the problem; interjecting summary points; interpreting nonverbal cues such as facial expressions; and providing some initial reaction.

> Critical listening helps others explore all sides of an issue.

Part of being a critical listener also involves letting the other person fully present their idea before passing a verbal or nonverbal response.

You should gently prod people for feedback

Professor Rob Gilbert teaches at Montclair State University. He's a wonderful man and a great teacher. He has the ability to creatively chide, coax, nudge, and push his students to keep them engaged in the material, helping them understand why the lessons are critical for their developmental needs and interests. He draws their active participation through questions, storytelling, videos, self-deprecating humor, complimentary and constructive comment, and with welcomed two-way communication.

There should be a little of Dr. Gilbert in all organizational leaders.

You may say, "I don't know;" however, then say, "I'll get back to you."

And do. On those occasions when an answer isn't available, be sure to follow up when a response is known—especially for those queries that deal with change. This will actively demonstrate your commitment to and trust with your team by taking their input seriously and reacting accordingly.

You should make sure that everyone's opinion is welcomed and respected

At a recent "town-hall meeting" at the ABC Company, an employee inquired why her team wasn't consulted earlier in a particular decision. The executive who the question was pointed to bluntly replied that if he wanted her opinion, he would ask. Further, the executive chastised the inquirer by summarily telling her to keep her mouth shut and to trust management.

How many more questions were asked after that public dressing-down?

To state the obvious, this approach is unacceptable. The employee was embarrassed, other participants were appalled, and a great collective learning opportunity was bypassed.

Oh, and the executive—for not embracing the question—looked like a fool.

TRUTH

42

Decision making:
The fastest don't always
finish first

We've all worked with managers who, rather than make a difficult decision, will procrastinate until the last possible minute—preferring the status quo or trying to sidestep potential conflict. By consequence, this absence of action often makes matters worse.

On the other hand, America's self-proclaimed CEO of the nineties, "Chainsaw" Al Dunlap, took Sunbeam Corporation to its knees with his failure to anticipate or manage the unraveling of his organization. He hastily made all the decisions—many before he walked in the door—and he reportedly listened to no one in the process.

In times of organizational change, you will be making dozens of decisions—gathering the facts, defining the problem, identifying available options, obtaining opinions, evaluating possible courses of action, and communicating and implementing a solution. Some decisions will be of little consequence; others will have a visible and pragmatic ripple effect for individuals as well as all organizational participants. You will wear many hats—from judge to referee—and the decision-making style you employ will be in a spotlight.

It may surprise you to know that the style that has served you so well in the past may not be an asset at this point in time. Recent research shows you must adjust your decision-making style as you climb your way up the corporate ladder—or risk missing a rung. Specifically, direct, command-oriented decision making is appropriate for the frontline supervisor on the shop floor. But through and for career progression, you must be open, seek input and opinion, welcome participation, and embrace a more flexible and collaborative style.

Here are some best practices to consider for decision making at any level within the organization.

Work the room ahead of time

Denis R. Brown, a retired executive from ITT and former CEO of Concurrent Computer Corporation, was a master at building consensus around decisions, and his inclusion methodology was straightforward and simple.

> You must adjust your decision-making style as you climb your way up the corporate ladder—or risk missing a rung.

On an ongoing basis, he contacted all board members to gather information and perspective about the critical issues for deliberation, as well as to give business updates. This served two primary purposes: It fortified his individual relationships with his key constituents, and the resulting insight helped him prepare for and manage these diverse opinions during discussion.

Not everyone left the boardroom agreeing with every decision; however, everyone understood why the decision was made and could support it.

Don't be afraid to make decisions

Jack Welch, the former CEO of General Electric, was hardly shy about making decisions. In his quest to make GE the "most valuable" company from an investor's perspective in the 1980s, he reorganized the company into a decentralized model focusing on service industries and eliminating unprofitable areas. His ultimate goal was to pare the organization, resulting in nearly 200,000 employees leaving GE—saving over $6 billion. Having then torn the company apart, he set out to rebuild GE into a "boundary-less" corporation with common values, an emphasis on quality through the introduction of "Six Sigma," proactive performance management, and enhanced communications and collaboration.

He was successful—very successful.

Act with appropriate haste

Time can be either an ally (such as when dealing with an emotionally charged issue) or an enemy (such as when your bottom line is bleeding).

Make your decisions with appropriate deliberation about what must be done, why, where, when, who, and how. Make every attempt to be fair and objective, thus minimizing political influence.

Once the decision is made, be sensitive to any humanistic aspects, and move forward with delivery and execution as soon as possible.

Know that your credibility is on the line every day

Try to avoid "maybe" answers, or follow up when time has presumably given more clarity to the situation.

Unless new information becomes available, stick to your word

Remember that trust is a byproduct of congruence between your words and actions. Execute your decisions and only revisit them if new information surfaces that might cause you to take another direction.

TRUTH

43

Exceptions:
Can't live with them;
can't live without them

For years, legal practitioners have told management to treat everyone the same. Use the same hiring practices, the same disciplinary considerations, and the same review processes for hires, transfers, and promotions. Pay everyone the same. Conform to legally compliant and consistently administered organizational policies and practices. Give little or no consideration to individual differences or circumstance.

Philosophically, the lawyers are absolutely right; however, pragmatically, they're wrong. There are good reasons to make exceptions. This is particularly true when you're asking your team to do more with less, work harder, work longer, and work smarter—all while they're trying to maintain a life outside of work.

When all people are treated the same, managers stifle creativity; smother innovation, and pigeon-hole individuals into defined and limited areas of contribution. Conversely, managers who arbitrarily or purposely look the other way run the risk of being accused of favoritism, while potentially setting in motion an unwanted impetus toward coworker grumbling and resentment.

When an employee raises the need for special treatment during times of extraordinary personal circumstance, hopefully, short-term adjustments may be designed and implemented to meet the needs of both parties.

When a request comes along that is counter to an accepted norm (that is, for flextime; telecommuting; working from home; extended time off; and participation on various committees and training initiatives), there are four primary considerations.

First and foremost, despite the temptation, never bend or break a rule for an individual if it compromises your business needs. This will undoubtedly cause an unwanted hiccup at some point—most likely at the least opportune time.

> **Never bend or break a rule for an individual if it compromises your business needs.**

If the request is for something out of the ordinary, consider why the ordinary is important. If it's not necessary, maybe the ordinary should be changed.

On the other hand, receptionists can't telecommute, and technical support needs to be available when the customers are in need.

Second, only consider exceptions for your exemplary performers.

For these individuals, initiate any work rule modifications on a trial basis, building in some conditions such as higher accountability in the case of telecommuting or flexible time. This will help ensure that the work is getting done. As appropriate, you can expect the employee to make up time that he misses and to document work product and time more than under "ordinary" circumstances. Written periodic reports and status updates on tasks and projects can be a reasonable substitute for drop-in Q&A and the face-to-face opportunities afforded in typical office settings.

Related to this, every member of the team should know that if they are contributing, they will be extended considerations that others have been accorded, as may be appropriate to their circumstances in the future.

Third, be prepared to explain to the rest of the team why you're making an exception. When doing so, it's a good opportunity to communicate the values hierarchy that led to the decision to grant the request. It's also important that all employees know that the exception isn't a change in policy but is appropriate under the specific circumstances and may not be appropriate for all situations.

Last, be sure that you aren't establishing an unwanted precedent for the organization and that your action passes legal scrutiny. If the decision process is well thought through, and communicated effectively, the risk here can be minimized. However, it makes sense to review the process with counsel; and in articulating the business reasons why the decision is appropriate, you can gain some protection against claims of bias.

> Be sure that you aren't establishing an unwanted precedent for the organization and that your action passes legal scrutiny.

Pam Poff is a well-known and highly accomplished attorney based in New Jersey. She provides sound guidance and training to global organizational leaders about employment law. Inevitably, she also gets a call when organizations get into trouble.

When Pam coaches and counsels in matters of employment practices (hiring, firing, promotions, reduction-in-force, discipline, accommodations, and so on), she refers to an OUCH paradigm. Specifically, she suggests that pending management decisions about these matters should be

- **O**bjective (measurable and quantifiable)
- **U**niformly applied
- **C**onsistent
- **H**ave a job-relatedness

If your answers to OUCH are "yes," then you're probably on safe legal grounds. Certainly, if there are gray areas, you may want to give your local Pam a shout—before you move ahead with any exceptions to the rules.

Note: The pointers in this section aren't intended to address the accommodation process required under state/federal law in the case of an individual with a handicap/disability.

TRUTH

44

Employee discipline:
Ask the more meaningful
question

How you publicly respond to mistakes of omission and commission is important in the eyes of your team.

At some point in your career, a coworker will knock on your office door to inform you of a sensitive employee relations matter involving a serious breach of company policy. This may involve rule "bending" well beyond any original intention, or behavior that isn't consistent with the organization's values. Examples include employee theft, merit review bias, quality shortcuts, sexual harassment, intellectual property "sharing," sales "loading," supplier "influence," and internal politics and backstabbing.

If you're lucky, the matter is another manager's mess to untangle, but what if it's yours?

When you're confronted with employee misconduct, you must first investigate the allegations. Begin by objectively gathering information. Speak to all involved parties and those with knowledge of the transgression. Protect confidentiality to the extent possible. Try to identify the scope of the problem—the critical path of events, accountabilities, actions, or decisions involved. Was this act prompted by ignorance or malicious intent? Was it defiance or a cry for help?

When your initial information gathering of the transgression is complete, you must consider the employee's work history, any extenuating circumstances, precedents, related training and education, and the implications for the balance of the team.

In the final stages of analysis, consider the consequences for inaction, the options for action, and the likely support of senior management.

Now comes decision-making time—weighing the pros and cons of alternatives. This is when you debate, "What should we do to the employee?"

Consult with your manager, as well as human resources. If the gravity of the situation calls for some type of discipline, your discussion will focus on how you wish to privately handle or publicly flog the involved parties—a frank discussion, a verbal or written warning, disciplinary probation, a suspension, or termination.

While your decision regarding the matter's response and any individual discipline is important, there is a concurrent concern that is of equal if not greater importance in your team's eyes. Yet, this concern is rarely raised in U.S. companies, for there is a bias for acting with haste to put the matter in the past tense.

This concern focuses upon this: What should we do for the employee?

During times of significant organizational change, your team members will have your every word and action under a microscope.

What should we do for the employee?

They will question your motives and approach. They may second-guess your decisions. What they can't speculate about is that you care.

Be appropriately respectful, compassionate, and humanistic when disciplining an employee. Even if your options for corrective measures are limited, your goal is to prevent a recurrence of the transgression. If the fault lies with ignorance, then individual or collective training or orientation may be a solution. If skills must be enhanced, perhaps education and mentoring are options. If time and attendance are part of the challenge, maybe a more flexible schedule can be enacted. If assigning a coach would help, it should be considered. If the matter is appropriate for public discussion so learning may occur, bring it into dialogue and make periodic references to it.

By offering ongoing remedies, the individuals involved will know that you consider them to be worthy of your time and attention. Consequently, they will be more likely to recover from any setbacks and be more prone to give you return on your investment.

Note: While you may lose sleep over decisions such as a reduction-in-force, don't let your nocturnal slumber be disrupted when you fire someone for serious breaches of company policy or values. These individuals have fired themselves.

TRUTH

45

Make every employee feel like your only employee

Intuition tells us that most people want to feel good about themselves, what they are doing, whom they work for, and what their organization stands for. They want to play an active role on a team, feel a sense of security, have an opportunity for socialization, and to build their individual confidence and esteem. In short, we all like to feel appreciated.

Unfortunately, most managers get caught up in the fire drills of each day, rarely taking or making the opportunity to "get to know" their team on an individual basis.

This can prove mutually detrimental. Team members may lose their sense of community, confidence and pride. Likewise, managers, in their zest to homogenize their team around shared vision, goals, values, and deliverables, may not have or gain a full appreciation for individual differences—inadvertently stifling opportunities for the ways that team members may grow, develop, and contribute.

Effective managers know that while each person's contribution may vary, every team member is important. They recognize that all people are unique—from their DNA to predisposition—in values, attitudes, and beliefs. They appreciate people as complex individuals, each with given talents and developmental needs. They view individuals as repositories for and assets of unique knowledge, skills, and life experience. They know that how we learn, what motivates us, factors concerning our job satisfaction, and how we prefer to be managed vary.

> All people are unique—from their DNA to predisposition—in values, attitudes, and beliefs.

Our ability to select, process, and respond to informational inputs within an environment characterized by sensory overload—such as rapid organizational change—is influenced by our own personal values, attitudes, and beliefs. Accordingly, we need to be conscious of our own systemic biases, recognizing that our own cognitive and emotional interpretations might filter the reality being presented. If we label others, we will treat them according to that label.

To build bridges with your team, you must have an open mind and be objective—appreciating and respecting the offerings and backgrounds of all parties, whatever their gender, age, religion, or heritage. You have to broaden your perspective. In a sincere manner, you must make everyone feel important. You must relate to each person differently and treat everyone with dignity by showing your genuine interest in them as individuals.

> You must have an open mind and be objective— appreciating and respecting the offerings and backgrounds of all parties, whatever their gender, age, religion, or heritage.

Here are some tips:

- Address colleagues on a first-name basis. Acknowledge birthdays and special personal events. Engage in some small talk about the kids, the weekend, the reunion, little league, or other outside interests, and occasionally surprise someone by taking her to lunch. This will demonstrate that you care.

- Treat each person in a mature manner by engaging with your team as adults capable of assessing and sharing risks.

- Embrace cultural sensitivity. For example, simple verbal communication across cultures has its challenges:

  "The English use understatement and reservations; they may be vague to avoid confrontation and to be polite. Spaniards, French, and Italians use language to be eloquent and expressive. Germans use logic. American speech tends to be direct and to the point. The Japanese use words that can sound like diplomatic platitudes, while their tone, gestures, and body language convey what they're really saying. Hard negotiating may be veiled in pleasantries, which can mislead the Westerner. In Asian cultures, 'yes' may mean, 'I understand'—not, 'I agree.'"

- Appreciate that people have different work style preferences (individual versus group); approaches (task versus relationship); and comfort levels with ambiguity.

- Be cognizant of the influence of one's generation upon an individual's world perspective. For example, in the United States, the economic, social, and political forces in one's formative years likely have had significant impact upon the individual's independence, institutional attitude, patience, and organizational loyalty. Case in point, a team member from the Baby Boomers generation sees the world through a different lens than a recent college graduate.

- Nurture a "culture of inclusion," being open to diverse styles, ideas, and perspectives. Involve others in the design of their work, offering learning opportunities, and drawing each individual into a dialogue about problem-solving.

Conclusively, recognize each person for how she contributes and why you can't do it without her.

TRUTH

46

A little formal recognition goes a long way

In his best-selling book, *Emotional Intelligence*, author Daniel Goleman cites the ease at which managers criticize an individual's performance—yet hold back on showing gratitude.

This is an important habit to break if you're a faulty praise practitioner.

Our ears enjoy a compliment. Often, it can make the difference in your attitude for the day. More so, as a motivational managerial tool, it can help you retain your best employees, as countless studies and workplace climate surveys indicate that paying attention to your team members, beyond money, is a significant key to their productivity and job satisfaction. In fact, the number one reason executives leave their jobs is a lack of praise and recognition.

As a manager, you must remember that everything you accomplish—change—is through people. And if you want to keep them happy and satisfied, recognizing your colleagues through expressions such as "Good job," "Way to go!" and "Thank you" must be a part of your verbal repertoire.

> The number one reason executives leave their jobs is a lack of praise and recognition.

These words should come across with forethought and sincerity.

When you catch a team member doing something right—no matter how relatively slight it may seem—personally acknowledge it as soon as possible. To the extent possible, personally convey the message.

Too many words too often may come across as superficial; too little too late, and the linkage between the action and the praise is lost.

Where you praise an individual is as important as the act itself.

Libby Sartain, former vice president of people at Southwest Airlines, recounts when one of their pilots, Roger Way, successfully avoided what would have been a sure tragedy by deftly landing a plane with inoperable landing gear. As the story is told, Captain Way happened to be visiting the company's headquarters shortly thereafter. When word spread that he was in the building, an impromptu gathering involving hundreds of their employees was arranged in the lobby.

This public event not only gave Captain Way recognition for his extraordinary efforts, but it helped to generate goodwill and promote team-building.

How you pay attention to employees, including addressing workplace environmental concerns, provides you with many options.

In the classic Hawthorne studies conducted by Elton Mayo from 1927 to 1932 at a Western Electric manufacturing plant outside Chicago, many workplace variables were altered (lighting, rest periods, payment incentives, supervisory styles, and so on) with increases in productivity and morale resulting. Mayo concluded that job satisfaction increased as workers were given more freedom; that interaction and cooperation created a high level of cohesiveness; and that job satisfaction and productivity depended more on a feeling of self-worth than environment.

What you praise individuals for should be of significance, and it should be consistent with the organization's values. This will reinforce the behavior and set a tone for others.

Related to this, you should take every opportunity to share and give credit—commemorating the accomplishment of significant accomplishments or milestones. But don't dwell here unless you're at a journey's end, as you will need to refresh and refocus the team.

Also, *the form of recognition* is important, and it need not be costly. For, while many companies have budgets for recognition programs with every bell and whistle imaginable, your personalized efforts might include a handshake, a note of thanks, taking an employee to lunch, giving a voucher good for "dinner for two," a service award, a gift certificate, a special bonus, or spontaneous time off. Outside of work, sending a birthday card, sending flowers for an appropriate occasion, or attending a personal event—like a wedding or funeral—is all very appropriate.

Recognition isn't the only organizational determinant of job satisfaction and employee motivation (as others include the relationships with one's supervisor and peers, the perceived quality of supervision, the work itself, social stimulation, personal engagement, and working conditions), but it's critical for your managerial success.

TRUTH

47

Your best investment is in...
YOU

If you're standing still, you're falling behind.

As we have touched upon, visible and subtle change is happening all around us all the time. It impacts our business, the marketplace, our relationships, our work processes and practices, and our need to get results. The way we anticipate change, plan for it, digest it, and respond to it must change as well.

Education is the great equalizer. It provides you with the credentials that should open doors and open minds. It generates energy and perspective. It gives you new ideas, levels of understanding, and an appreciation for business complexities. In the best case, it also teaches you how to apply what you've learned.

Education is the great equalizer.

But hitting the books isn't enough. You must explore other areas of continuous learning.

Anticipate

If you still use a VCR, you're in the slow lane. If it still blinks 12:00, that's a bigger problem.

Try to anticipate the next resource needs of your organization (technology, people, equipment, materials, services, and so on) and their potential organizational application. If possible, get ahead on the learning curve.

Be a consummate reader

On a daily basis, grab the newspaper and stay abreast of the day's business and political and headlines. Also, getting to the bookstore or browsing the Internet should allow you to find materials where you can refresh, close information gaps, or get acquainted within your function or industry.

Have curiosity

"What's become clear since we last met?" is a quote attributed to Ralph Waldo Emerson. These few words outline the philosophical underpinning for life-long personal growth and professional development through curiosity and engagement.

Generally speaking, successful leaders have a natural curiosity about the organization that causes them to ask questions aimed at improving operational effectiveness and efficiency. If you do not have such curiosity, it would be wise to list this as an area for development, as it will serve you well in the long term.

Stay "linked" to your customer

Although very successful in the television industry, Andy Hill will be the first to tell you that he's a bit of a Hollywood outsider.

Several summers ago, Andy accompanied his son Aaron to a music arts camp in Michigan. In doing so, Andy, along with 1,500 young adults and 2,500 others of parenting age, attended the camp's Fourth of July concert. As the conductor introduced the traditional service academy songs, he invited all of the veterans in the audience to stand and be recognized. As the veterans rose, the 1,500 young adults spontaneously erupted into a standing ovation. There was likely not a dry eye to be found.

Why is this important? As Andy suggests, this was the target audience for the quality shows he was providing oversight for at CBS in the 1990s (*Touched by an Angel, Walker, Texas Ranger, and Dr. Quinn, Medicine Woman*). It wasn't for executives in New York and Los Angeles, but for the Midwestern folks with heartland values that he was rubbing elbows with on a steamy July night. Presumably, had Andy stayed within the confines of Hollywood that July, he would have missed both the personal bond of sharing that moment with his son, as well as the important input from the people whom his programming efforts were intended for.

Join professional associations

Pursue appropriate memberships and attend professional meetings. These are great opportunities for informational and experiential exchange.

Pursue training opportunities

A motivational speaker once asked an audience of mid-career professionals if they knew the difference between "training" and "education."

When no hands were raised, the speaker then asked how many in the audience were parents of teenagers. Many people nodded.

He then asked those parents if they preferred for their children to be taking a course titled "sexual education" or "sexual training."

His point was made.

Training represents the transfer of knowledge or skill. In attending various training courses—for leadership, technical proficiency, or personal effectiveness—your challenge is to convert the course materials to action—as opposed to allowing them to collect dust on a shelf.

Keep your network alive

As previously mentioned, keep a small trusted circle of external advisors and counselors in your address book. Reach out as needed. Better yet, advise them on how best they can help you. Likewise, certain coworkers can provide expertise, opinion, or assistance in reading the cultural tea leaves.

Be bold

Jim Whittaker, the first American to climb Mount Everest, observed, "You never conquer the mountain. You conquer yourself—your doubts and your fears."

What are your professional fears, and how will you tackle them?

48

Your title is manager; your job is teacher

As much as you may think or hope, sending your adolescent child to a sports camp for a couple weeks doesn't necessarily mean that he or she will be the next Michael Jordan or Billie Jean King.

This same principle holds true at work.

As a manager, you have a vested interest in enhanced employee proficiency and shared learning. These are prerequisites for the production of high-quality products and services. When all team members are skilled and qualified in the activities and processes they're required to perform, there will be fewer errors/corrections, higher productivity, and greater employee satisfaction/morale.

Your challenge in this regard is twofold: to determine whom to invest in and how much.

> Your challenge in this regard is twofold: to determine whom to invest in and how much.

Start by selecting the "right" people to develop.

Within your organization, there are people dedicated to the customer. They have a results-orientation. They're technically competent and have a high aptitude for learning. Their attributes include enthusiasm, a desire to make a difference, commitment, and the highest standards for excellence. They're your best performers. They welcome "stretch" objectives.These are the employees—your "A" players, who deserve your time and attention.

How do you invest in these people?

First, consider the learning methodology preferred by the individual. People learn and become motivated in different ways—including seeing and reading; listening and speaking; and touching and doing. Work with each individual to determine his strength and maximize the opportunity for learning accordingly. For example, kinesthetic learners favor special projects, committee involvement, job sharing, job rotation, shadowing, simulations and modeling, and role-playing. On the other hand, visual learners prefer independent learning, case studies, classroom experience, observation, learning maps, study sabbaticals, and white papers.

Second, share and apply the learning.

Comedian Sam Levenson once stated, "You must learn from the mistakes of others. You can't possibly live long enough to make them all yourself."

Case in point, Tom Watson, Sr., IBM's founder, handled a promising executive's failed business gamble not by firing him but by suggesting that the company had just invested $10 million—the cost of his business blunder—in his education. Watson understood that experience is the best teacher and that individual and collective learning may be derived from failure and success alike.

Third, learn how to teach.

Legendary UCLA basketball coach John Wooden has a wonderful sign over his desk that reads, "It's what you learn after you know it all that counts."

Quite an instructor in his own right, Wooden pushed hard and demanded the most. He boiled teaching down to four basic components that are universal in application:

- **Demonstration**—This is providing someone with a pragmatic example to follow. Be it how to bank a 15-foot jumper or how to make a sales cold call, followers are shown or told of the proper technique to execute their responsibilities. For this step to have maximum effectiveness, leaders must provide rationale, tools, and related resources.

- **Imitation**—This involves initial trial, trying to reproduce and apply what has been demonstrated.

- **Correction**—This entails enhanced trial, with the goal of eliminating deviations.

- **Repetition**—This requires performing the task over and over, striving for quality and perfection with each attempt.

These four components may be used for teaching basketball, the alphabet, skilled carpentry, and finance. Use them, embrace them, and share them.

Fourth, provide appropriate encouragement.

In a recent interview, former New York Giant quarterback Phil Simms touched on the topic of encouragement. It seemed Phil was taking the field before a big game, feeling some anticipatory jitters—which became amplified as his fiery coach, Bill Parcells, approached him.

However, rather than the coach badgering Phil of his day's "to-do's," Parcells told Phil that if he did not throw at least a couple of interceptions, he would not be trying hard enough.

That comment broke the tension, instilled confidence, and provided encouragement for Simms to put forth the needed effort.

TRUTH

49

Trying to be all things to all people is a slippery slope

Did you know that Karoh-shi is the Japanese word meaning "death by overwork," and it's recognized as a cause of mortality?

Alex was hired into a position of significant organizational authority. New to this role, he could say "no" to no one, and he devoted the majority of his waking hours to his work—trying to quickly make a name. Unfortunately, he also held others to this standard and publicly berated those who failed to do so. It got to the point, over time, where nervous breakdowns, anxiety attacks, and increased absenteeism and turnover on his team became the rules—not the exceptions.

Despite numerous interventions by head of human resources and threats by the CEO, Alex's promises to amend his ways were empty. In fact, he pushed himself and those remaining even harder. As further consequence, not only did his once-promising career suffer a major setback (as he was eventually terminated), but also his largely ignored personal life also crashed and burned. Three marriages, children with significant drug issues, legal mishaps, ethical lapses, and health concerns all transpired. Ultimately, he relocated to other pastures, running from a closet full of skeletons.

Alex's mistakes were many, but the root cause of his problems was his inability to identify and focus on what should have been his main concerns.

While it sounds easy to prioritize your time and attention, it's not. Many parties and interests, in many directions, are pulling at you during times of change—inside and outside of work. This is why you must be concerned with where and how you're spending your time.

> Many parties and interests, in many directions, are pulling at you during times of change—inside and outside of work.

Where your time is spent may be addressed with a threefold approach.

First, take a brief personal inventory of how you spend your time—on and off the job—from the alarm clock's call. Allowing time for eating, grooming, and some basic chores, you may be surprised at some of the findings when you look at a week's snapshot.

Second, on a daily basis, make a to-do list—ranking activities in terms of importance and urgency, and allowing some time for crisis management. Anticipate deadlines and practice self-discipline. Try to stick to the list. This can keep you on task and give you a sense of accomplishment as activities are completed.

Third, on a longer term basis, avoid spreading yourself too thin by making an index card your best friend. On this card, list your key five or six current life priorities (family, work, school, professional development, gym time, piano, fishing, and so on) and place the card in a visible place by your desk. Refer to it frequently. If where you are spending the majority of your time isn't on or related to this prioritized list, why are you doing it?

You may actually find this index card exercise to be personally invigorating, particularly if you involve others in the creation process.

As far as how your time is spent, you need to manage peaks and valleys (everything can't be a fire drill) and hone your skills of delegation.

Delegation is critical. It helps you develop your team and ultimately plan for succession. It also helps people grow and become motivated. Finally, it helps you balance your workload, as well as others'.

> You need to manage peaks and valleys (everything can't be a fire drill) and hone your skills of delegation.

To delegate effectively, you must be comfortable in giving up control (though not responsibility) for a task. You must also have confidence in the ability of others to help. Like all areas of performance management, this involves assigning the task, setting expectations, providing resources, outlining timetables, and establishing feedback loops.

Delegation initially works best for simple tasks. As your faith and confidence grow in others, you may delegate more complex assignments. Be sure to ask the individual if she's comfortable with the responsibility and authority that you're giving. Your range of

195

delegation runs the gamut of asking someone to analyze a situation to having her determine and implement the corrective measures necessary.

Closing Thoughts

Bob Dylan was right then, and he is right now: The Times They Are A-Changin'.

These turbulent times demand a range of professional challenges and accountabilities. For management, you must provide purpose, set direction, organize and engage followers, enhance performance and productivity, and get results. Managing change is complex, fast-paced, and dynamic, and it involves many activities such as coaching, supervising, and disciplining. By role, it may be described with equal parts of words and actions.

The purpose of this book is to dispel some of the myths about managing organizational change by blending some how-to human resources guidance with contemporary research. It's my sincere hope that I've accomplished these outcomes and that you will join me in constantly pushing the envelope to find and share ways to make us better managers, and by consequence, to make our workplaces more satisfying, enjoyable, and productive.

Providing context

Bennis, W. G., & Nanus, B. (1997). *Leaders: Strategies for Taking Charge* (Second ed.). New York: HarperCollins Publishers, Inc., p. 129.

Covey, S. (1990). *The 7 Habits of Highly Effective People.* New York: Simon & Schuster, p. 287.

Truth 1

AIS: The American Institute of Stress. "Job stress." Retrieved February 9, 2007 from www.stress.org

Cohen, J. M. (2007). "The Brain and New Age Rhetoric," JM Cohen Associates Journal, Volume 4, No. 2., p.4.

Heathfield, S. M. "Understanding Stress and Workplace Stress." Retrieved March 13, 2007 from http://humanresources.about.com/od/stressandtimemanagement/a/stress_time.htm

Truth 2

Bennis, W. G., & Nanus, B. (1997). *Leaders: Strategies for Taking Charge* (Second ed.). New York: HarperCollins Publishers, Inc., p. 37–39.

Coles, R. (2001). *Lives of Moral Leadership: Men and Women Who Have Made a Difference.* New York: Random House, p. 129.

Kouzes, J. M., & Posner, B. Z. (1995). *The Leadership Challenge: How to Get Extraordinary Things Done in Organizations.* San Francisco, CA: Jossey-Bass Inc., Publishers, p. 214.

Kuczmarski, S. S. & Kuczmarski, T.D. (1995). *Values-based Leadership: Rebuilding Employee Commitment, Performance & Productivity.* Englewood Cliffs, NJ: Prentice Hall, Inc., p. 109.

Long, S. (2002). *Competitive Intelligence: An Organizational Development Initiative Regarding Performance Enhancement, Leadership Development and Cultural Transformation.* Colorado Springs, CO: Motere Institute, p. 22.

Smye, M. (1998). *Is It Too Late to Run Away and Join the Circus? A Guide for Your Second Life.* New York: Macmillan Publishing, p. 73.

Truth 3

Bolles, R. N. (1996). *What Color Is Your Parachute?* Berkeley, CA: Ten Speed Press, p. 174–175.

Cho, J. Lessons in employee appreciation. *The Star-Ledger.* February 8, 2007, p. 51.

Musbach, T. "Many workers to consider new jobs in 2007." Retrieved January 3, 2007 from http://hotjobs.promotions.yahoo.com/cci/article.php)

Sartain, L., & Finney, M. (2003). *HR from the Heart.* American Management Association: New York, p. 36–37, 78–81.

Truth 4

Watkins, M. (2003). *The First 90 Days.* Boston, MA: Harvard Business School Publishing. p. 216–223.

Watts, P. M. (2007, February). The Annual Human Resources Roundtable—2007. The chief human resource officer—achieving success in the first 100 days (lecture notes). Sponsored by HRD Consultants and Philosophy IB. The Princeton Club: New York.

Truth 5

Hackman, J. R. (2002) *Leading Teams: Setting the Stage for Great Performances.* Boston, MA: Harvard Business School Press, p. 223–225.

Truth 6

Kotter, J. P. (1996). *Leading Change.* Boston, MA: Harvard Business School. p. 25–31.

Truth 7

"Attitudes drive behavior." Retrieved March 19, 2007 from http://www.as.wvu.edu/~sbb/comm221/chapters/abc.htm. September 15, 1996; Copyright SBB, 1996.

Bennis, W. G., et al. (advisory board) (2002). *Business: The Ultimate Resource.* Cambridge, MA: Perseus Publishing, p. 1152–1153.

Hiam, A. (2003). *Motivational Management.* American Management Association: New York, p. 28–31; 82–83, 160–163.

Truth 8

Hyland, P. (personal communication, July 4, 2006).

Pelligrini, F. (2002). "Person of the Week: 'Enron Whistleblower'" Sherron Watkins. *Time Magazine* in partnership with CNN, January 18. Retrieved July 1, 2007 from http://www.time.com/time/printout/0,8816,194927,00.html

Pritchett, P., & Pound, R. (1993). *High-velocity Culture Change—A Handbook for Managers.* Dallas, Texas: Pritchett & Associates, Inc., p. 24.

Society for Human Resource Management (global forum). 2002 Global Leadership Survey, Alexandria, VA.

Truth 9

Watkins, M. (2003). *The First 90 Days.* Boston, MA: Harvard Business School Publishing.

Truth 10

Sartain, L., & Finney, M. (2003). *HR from the Heart.* American Management Association: New York. p. 28–29.

Watkins, M. (2003). *The First 90 Days.* Boston, MA: Harvard Business School Publishing. p. 106–113.

Truth 11

Friedman, T. L. (2006). *The World Is Flat: A Brief History of the Twenty-First Century.* New York: Farrer, Straus and Giroux.

Truth 14

Bennis, W. G., & Townsend, R. (1995). *Reinventing Leadership: Strategies to Empower the Organization.* New York: William Morrow Company, p. 37.

Collins, J. C. (2001). *Good to Great: Why Some Companies Make the Leap and Others Don't.* New York: HarperCollins Publishers, Inc., p. 118–119.

Ellsworth, R. R. (2002). *Leading with Purpose.* Stanford, CA: Stanford University Press. p. 97.

Hamel, G., & Prahalad, C. K. (1994). *Competing for the Future: Breakthrough Strategies for Seizing Control of Your Industry and Creating the Markets for Tomorrow.* Boston, MA: Harvard Business School Press, p. 16–17.

Kotter, J. P. (1996). *Leading Change.* Boston, MA: Harvard Business School, p. 68–69, 72.

Kouzes, J. M., & Posner, B. Z. (1995). *The Leadership Challenge: How to Get Extraordinary Things Done in Organizations.* San Francisco, CA: Jossey-Bass Inc., Publishers, p. 97, 124.

White, R. March 29, 2007, private conversation.

Truth 15

Badaracco, J. L., & Ellsworth, R. R (1989). *Leadership and the Quest for Integrity.* Boston, MA: Harvard Business School Press, p. 49.

Mercer Delta Consulting, LLC. (1998). "The congruence model: a roadmap for understanding organizational performance." *Mercer Delta Insights.* New York: Mercer Delta Consulting, LLC, p. 6.

Price Waterhouse Change Integration Team. (1995). *Better Change: Best Practices for Transforming Your Organization.* New York: Irwin Professional Publishing. p. 7–10.

Tregoe, B., Zimmerman, J. W., Smith, R.A., & Tobia, P. (1989). *Vision in Action: Putting a Winning Strategy to Work.* New York: Simon & Schuster, p. 38.

Truth 16

Hiam, A. (2003). *Motivational Management.* New York: American Management Association, p. 89.

Price Waterhouse Change Integration Team. (1995). *Better Change: Best Practices for Transforming Your Organization.* New York: Irwin Professional Publishing. p. 15–21.

Truth 17

Bennis, W. G. et al. (advisory board). (2002). *Business: The Ultimate Resource.* Cambridge, MA: Perseus Publishing, p. 1044.

Blanchard, K., & O'Connor, M. (1997). *Managing by Values.* San Francisco, CA: Berrett-Koehler Publishers, Inc., p. 39–44.

Coles, R. (2001). *Lives of Moral Leadership: Men and Women Who Have Made a Difference*. New York: Random House, p. 129.

Collins, J., & Porras, J. I. (2002). *Built to Last: Successful Habits of Visionary Companies*. New York: HarperCollins Publishers, Inc., p. 48.

Collins, J. C. (2001). *Good to Great: Why Some Companies Make the Leap and Others Don't*. New York: HarperCollins Publishers, Inc., p. 195.

Gittell, J. H. (2003). *The Southwest Airlines Way*, McGraw-Hill, New York, p. 42.

Kouzes, J. M., & Posner, B. Z. (1995). *The Leadership Challenge: How to Get Extraordinary Things Done in Organizations*. San Francisco, CA: Jossey-Bass Inc., Publishers, p. 213–215.

Kuczmarski, S. S., & Kuczmarski, T. D. (1995). *Values-based Leadership: Rebuilding Employee Commitment, Performance & Productivity*. Englewood Cliffs, NJ: Prentice Hall, Inc., p. 53–58.

Maister, D. (1997). *True Professionalism: The Courage to Care About Your People, Your Clients, and Your Career*. New York: The Free Press, p. 75.

Pride, D. T. (1994 est.). *A Values Based Approach to Creating Alignment in Organizations*. Centre for Enabling Leadership. Goring on Thames, Oxfordshire, England, p. x, 3.

Truth 18

Bennis, W. G., & Townsend, R. (1995). *Reinventing Leadership: Strategies to Empower the Organization*. New York: William Morrow Company, p. 130–136.

Catell, R. B., Moore, K., & Rifkin, G. (2004). *The CEO and The Monk: One Company's Journey to Profit and Purpose*. New York: John Wiley & Sons, Inc.

O'Toole, J. (1996). *Leading Change—The Argument for Values-Based Leadership*. New York: Ballantine Books, p. 74–75.

Truth 19

Crawford, V. (1988). *From Confucius to Oz*. Singapore; Landmark Books. p. 80.

Truth 20

Price Waterhouse Change Integration Team. (1995). *Better Change: Best Practices for Transforming Your Organization.* New York: Irwin Professional Publishing. p. 81–91.

Tubbs, S. L., & Moss, S. (1977). *Human communication.* New York: Random House, Inc., p. 13.

Truth 21

Farace, R. V., Monge, P. R., & Russell, H. M. (1977). *Communicating and Organizing.* Reading, MA: Addison-Wesley Publishing Company, p. 104–125.

Lewis, K. R. (March 9, 2007). "Mental overload." *The Star-Ledger,* p. 35, 39.

Truth 22

Kotter, J. P. (1996). *Leading Change.* Boston, MA: Harvard Business School, p. 115.

Kouzes, J. M., & Posner, B. Z. (1995). *The Leadership Challenge: How to Get Extraordinary Things Done in Organizations.* San Francisco, CA: Jossey-Bass Inc., Publishers, p. 124–126.

Truth 23

Bjelland, O. M. (1994). Organizing for global renewal. *The Performance Agenda—Managing Change in the New Economy.* Oslo, Norway: The Performance Group, p. 51–64.

DePree, M. (1992). *Leadership Jazz.* New York: Bantam Doubleday Dell Publishing Group, Inc., p. 26–32.

Hamel, G., & Prahalad, C. K. (1994). *Competing for the Future: Breakthrough Strategies for Seizing Control of Your Industry and Creating the Markets for Tomorrow.* Boston, MA: Harvard Business School Press, p. 66.

Mercer Delta Consulting, LLC. (1998). "The Congruence Model: A Roadmap for Understanding Organizational Performance." *Mercer Delta Insights.* New York: Mercer Delta Consulting, LLC, p. 2–8.

Price Waterhouse Change Integration Team. (1995). *Better Change: Best Practices for Transforming Your Organization.* New York: Irwin Professional Publishing, p. 105–107.

Truth 24

Haigh, W. T. (1996). "Effective retention strategies." Overview presented at the annual conference for the International Association of Corporate and Professional Recruitment, Philadelphia, p. 4.

Hamel, G., & Prahalad, C. K. (1994). *Competing for the Future: Breakthrough Strategies for Seizing Control of Your Industry and Creating the Markets for Tomorrow*. Boston, MA: Harvard Business School Press, p. 245.

Smart, B. D., & Smart, G. H. (1997). "Topgrading the organization." *Directors & Boards*. Spring.

Watkins, M. (2003). *The First 90 Days*. Boston, MA: Harvard Business School Publishing, p. 162–167, 170–171.

Truth 25

Bennis, W. G. et al. (advisory board). (2002). *Business: The Ultimate Resource*. Cambridge, MA: Perseus Publishing, p. 1125.

Sartain, L., & Finney, M. (2003). *HR from the Heart*. American Management Association: New York. p. 106–107.

Truth 26

Lockwood, P. J. (personal communication, March 30, 2007).

Tomassi, K. D. "Most common resume lies." Forbes.com. Retrieved May 23, 2006 from http://www.forbes.com/2006/05/20/resume-lies-work_cx_kdt_06work_0523lies_print.html

Truth 27

Grove, C., & Hallowell, W. (2002). "Diversity in business." Alexandria, VA: Society for Human Resource Management. Retrieved in June from http://shrm.org/hrresources/whitepapers_published/CMS_000235.asp#P-4_0

Hastings, R. (2006). "Research shows business benefits from diversity." Alexandria, VA: Society for Human Resource Management. August, p. 1. Retrieved from www.shrm.org/diversity/library-published/nonIC/CMS_018181.asp.

D. Pelz, "Some Social Factors Related to Performance in a Research Organization," *Administrative Science Quarterly*, Vol. 1, 1956.

L. Hoffman & N. Maier, "Quality and Acceptance of Problem Solutions by Members of Homogeneous and Heterogeneous Groups," *Journal of Abnormal and Social Psychology*, Vol. 62, 1961.

D. Hambrick & P. Mason, "Upper Echelons: The Organization as a Reflection of Top Managers," *Academy of Management Review*, Vol. 9, 1984.

P. McLeod & S. Lobel, "Effects of Ethnic Diversity on Idea Generation in Small Groups," paper presented at the annual meeting of the Academy of Management, 1992.

W. Watson et al., "Cultural Diversity's Impact on Process and Performance," *Academy of Management Journal*, Vol. 36, 1993.

Truth 28

Bliss, W. G. (2004). "Executive assimilation." Alexandria, VA: Society of Human Resource Management, November.

Truth 29

Downs, A. "Downsizing with dignity: more pitfalls of downsizing." Retrieved March 13, 2006 from http://humanresources.about.com/od/layoffsdownsizing/a/downsizing_2.htm

Downs, A. "Downsizing with dignity: you can downsize with care—for people and the business." Retrieved March 13, 2006 from http://humanresources.about.com/od/layoffsdownsizing/a/downsizing.htm

Gittell, J. H. (2003). *The Southwest Airlines Way*. New York: McGraw-Hill, p. 243.

Sartain, L., & Finney, M. (2003). *HR from the Heart*. New York: American Management Association, p. 224–228.

Truth 30

NJ Department of Personnel (July 1998). Certified Public Managers Program, Learner's Guide, Module 3, p. 12 of 46.

Schaeffer, L. D. (October 2002). "The Leadership Journey." *Harvard Business Review*. p. 42–47.

Society for Human Resource Management (2005). *The SHRM Learning System*, Section 3: Alexandria, VA: Human Resources Development.

Truth 31

Arul, M. J. "Powers of power." Institute of Rural Management, Anand. Retrieved March 20, 2007 from http://members.tripod.com/~arulmj/powers.html

Hackman, J. R. (2002). *Leading Teams: Setting the Stage for Great Performances.* Boston, MA: Harvard Business School Press, p. 154–155.

McClelland, D. C., & Burnham, D. H. (1976). "Power is the great motivator." *Harvard business review*, 54 (2); p. 100–110 as noted by Arul.

Truth 32

Buckingham, M. (March 2005). "What great managers do." *Harvard business review*, p. 72.

Gittell, J. H. (2003). *The Southwest Airlines Way.* New York: McGraw-Hill, p. 204.

Hackman, J. R. (2002) *Leading Teams: Setting the Stage for Great Performances.* Boston, MA: Harvard Business School Press, p. 95.

Price Waterhouse Change Integration Team (1995). *Better Change: Best Practices for Transforming Your Organization.* New York: Irwin Professional Publishing. p. 171–181.

Sirota, D., Mischkind, L. A., and Meltzer, M. I. (January 2006). "Stop demotivating your employees!" *Harvard management update*, 11 (1), p. 1.

Townsend, P., & Gebhardt, J. (1997). *Five-Star Leadership: The Art and Strategy of Creating Leaders at Every Level.* New York: John Wiley & Sons, Inc., p. 131.

Truth 33

Bacal, R. (2000–2006). "Performance enhancement: diagnosing performance problems." Retrieved from http://performance-appraisals.org/Bacalsappraisalarticles/articles/diagper.htm

Carnegie, D. (1981). *How to Win Friends and Influence People.* (Second ed.). New York: Pocket Books, p. 207-208.

Truth 34

Hiam, A. (2003). *Motivational Management.* New York: American Management Association, p. 188–208.

Truth 35

Keenan, F., Welch, D., Black, J., & Fairlamb, D. (April 7, 2003). "Buyout pacts that backfire." *Business Week*, p. 68.

Sinha, R. (personal communication, February 2, 2007).

Ligos, M. (January 5, 2003). "Executive life: boot camps on ethics ask the 'what ifs.'" *The New York Times*, 3, p. 12.

Truitt, M. R. (1991). *The Supervisor's Handbook: Techniques for Getting Results Through Others.* National Press Publications, a Division of Rockhurst College Continuing Education Center, Inc.

Truth 36

Gittell, J. H. (2003). *The Southwest Airlines Way.* New York: McGraw-Hill, p. 251.

"JetBlue cancels flights, to present 'Bill of Rights'." CNN. Retrieved on February 19, 2007 from http://money.cnn.com/2007/02/19/news/companies/jetblue/index.htm?eref=rss_topstories

Kouzes, J. M., & Posner, B. Z (1995). *The Leadership Challenge: How to Get Extraordinary Things Done in Organizations.* San Francisco, CA: Jossey-Bass Inc., Publishers, p. 165, 220–223.

McGaw, N., & Fabish, L. (January 2006). "Put Your Values to Work." *Harvard Management Update*, 11 (1), p. 9–10.

Truth 37

Dulye, L. (June 2006). "Get out of your office." *HR magazine*, p. 99–101.

Priest, D., & Hull, A. (February 18, 2007). "Soldiers face neglect, frustration at army's top medical facility." *Washington Post*, A-1.

Truth 38

Mas, A., & Moretti, E. "Peers at work." UC Berkeley and NBER. Retrieved August 2006 from http://www.stanford.edu/group/SITE/Web%20Session%207/Moretti_Paper.pdf

Spencer, L. M., McClelland, D. C., & Spencer, S. M. (1994). *Competency Assessment Methods: History and State of the Art.* Hay McBer Research Press.

Truth 39

Beccaria, D. (November 15, 2005). "Managing conflict." Presented at Kyowa Pharmaceutical Inc. as part of a personal effectiveness training module sponsored by Rutgers University, Princeton, NJ.

Hambrick, D., & Mason, P. (1984). "Upper echelons: the organization as a reflection of top managers." *Academy of Management Review*, 9. As noted by Grove & Hallowell, 2002, p. 1, 2.

"How to resolve conflicts at work." Retrieved on March 20, 2007 from http://www.ehow.com/how_3820_resolve-conflicts-work.html

Kilman, T., "Conflict Resolution Grid," Copyright 1993-1997; Adaptation of Kilman Grid by Pepperdine University Straus Institute for Dispute Resolution. Retrieved from http://www.nccmpi.org/assets/Nina_Lunch.pdf on August 20, 2007.

Wheeler, T. "Choosing a conflict management style." Ohio Commission on Dispute Resolution and Conflict Management. Retrieved in 1995 from http://disputeresolution.ohio.gov/schools/contentpages/styles.htm

Truth 40

Kouzes, J. M., & Posner, B. Z. (1995). *The Leadership Challenge: How to Get Extraordinary Things Done in Organizations*. San Francisco, CA: Jossey-Bass Inc., Publishers, p. 152–164.

Truth 41

Adams, M. (2004). *Change Your Questions, Change Your Life*. San Francisco, CA: Berrett-Koehler Publishers, Inc.

NJ Department of Personnel, Certified Public Managers Program, Learner's Guide. (July 1998). Module 2, p. 15–17 of 47.

Truth 42

Bennis, W. G. et al. (advisory board). (2002). *Business: The Ultimate Resource*. Cambridge, MA: Perseus Publishing, p. 1156–1157.

Brousseau, K. R., Driver, M. J., Hourihan, G., & Larsson, R. (February 2006). "The seasoned executive's decision-making style." *Harvard Business Review*, p. 113.

"Chainsaw Al: he anointed himself America's best CEO. But Al Dunlap drove Sunbeam into the ground." *Business Week Online*. Retrieved

October 18, 1999 from http://www.businessweek.com/1999/99_42/b3651099.htm

Truitt, M. R. (1991). *The Supervisor's Handbook: Techniques for Getting Results Through Others.* National Press Publications, a Division of Rockhurst College Continuing Education Center, Inc.

Truth 43

Poff, P. (2006). "Legal issues." Presentation notes from Kyowa Pharmaceutical, Inc., Princeton, NJ, May 13, as part of KPI/Rutgers University Leadership Development Program.

Freeman, T. (personal communication, February 27, 2007).

White, R. (personal communication, February 27, 2007).

Truth 44

Messina, J. J., & Messina, C. M. (1999–2007). "Tools for relationships: productive problem solving." Retrieved from http://www.coping.org/relations/problem.htm

NJ Department of Personnel, Certified Public Managers Program, Learner's Guide (July 1998). Module 12, p 14 of 19.

Pritchett, P., & Pound, R. (1993). *High-Velocity Culture Change: A Handbook for Managers.* Dallas, Texas: Pritchett & Associates, Inc., p. 8.

Truth 45

Cohen, J. M. (2004). "When Cultures Collide," *JM Cohen Associates Journal,* 2 (3), p. 3

Grove, C., & Hallowell, W. (2002). "Diversity in business." Society for Human Resource Management, Alexandria, VA. Retrieved in June from http://shrm.org/hrresources/whitepapers_published/CMS_000235.asp#P-4_0

Truth 46

Goleman, D. (1995). "Emotional Intelligence." New York: Bantam Books, p. 152–153.

Kouzes, J. M., & Posner, B. Z. (1995). *The Leadership Challenge: How to Get Extraordinary Things Done in Organizations.* San Francisco, CA: Jossey-Bass Inc., Publishers, p. 270.

Bennis, W. G. et al. (advisory board). (2002). *Business: The Ultimate Resource.* Cambridge, MA: Perseus Publishing, p. 1020–1021.

Sartain, L., & Finney, M. (2003). *HR from the Heart.* American Management Association: New York. p. 179–180.

Truth 47

Bennis, W. G., & Nanus, B. (1997). *Leaders: Strategies for Taking Charge* (Second ed.). New York: HarperCollins Publishers, Inc., p. xv, 176.

Kouzes, J. M., & Posner, B. Z. (1995). *The Leadership Challenge: How to Get Extraordinary Things Done in Organizations.* San Francisco, CA: Jossey-Bass Inc., Publishers, p. 324.

Truth 48

Bennis, W. G., & Nanus, B. (1997). *Leaders: Strategies for Taking Charge* (Second ed.). New York: HarperCollins Publishers, Inc., p. 70.

Burke, R. A. (Reviewed 2002). "Strengthen your nucleus: manage the careers of high performing employees." Society for Human Resource Management, Alexandria, VA. Retrieved in July, 2007 from http://www.shrm.org/hrresources/whitepapers_published/CMS_000427.asp.

Chapman, A. (2005) www.businessballs.com

Communications Briefings, XXII (1), p. 8.

Wooden, J.R. (personal communication, August 22, 2002).

Truth 49

"Delegation: delegating authority skills, tasks and the process of effective delegation." Retrieved on April 5, 2007 from http://www.businessballs.com/delegation.htm

NJ Department of Personnel, Certified Public Managers Program, Learner's Guide. (July 1998). Module 8, p. 6 of 31.

About the Author

William S. Kane is a highly accomplished human resources executive with experience in all aspects of global functional management. He has specific expertise in leading, planning, and executing the human capital strategy associated with profitable business transformations—including startups, large-scale mergers and acquisitions, and enterprise-wide stabilization and repositioning.

Bill has held senior positions for a variety of multinational industrial leaders, such as International Flavors and Fragrances Inc., Electrolux/ Frigidaire, and FMC Corporation—companies with sales volumes ranging from $250 million to $17 billion, with more than 100,000 employees. He's presently the vice president of human resources and general administration for Kyowa Pharmaceutical in Princeton, NJ.

Bill is an adjunct professor in the MAOB graduate-level certificate program in leadership studies at Fairleigh Dickinson University, as well as a frequent guest lecturer at Montclair State University and at Rutgers University. His professional memberships include the New Jersey Human Resource Planning Group (NJHRPG), the Society for Human Resource Management (SHRM), and the national Academy of Management (AOM). He's also a mentor in the nationally recognized leadership program for Women Unlimited and in the Beyond the Banks executive program at Rutgers College.

Bill's perspective on matters of corporate responsibility and human resources has been featured in *USA Today*, *National Business Employment Weekly*, and *The Financial Times*. He has also appeared at New Jersey gubernatorial press conferences, New Jersey congressional hearings, and at forums sponsored by the New Jersey Department of Labor and the New Jersey Network.

Bill is currently studying for his Ph.D. in human and organization development at the Fielding Graduate University in Santa Barbara, California. As an extension of his academic efforts, Bill has collaborated with John Wooden, UCLA's Coach Emeritus, and Andy Hill, authors of the best-selling book *Be Quick But Don't Hurry*, to create and conduct management training seminars for corporate clients, civic groups, and students seeking to lead their teams toward optimized and sustained performance (www.woodenwayleadership.com).

Bill holds three master's degrees: an MA from Fielding in human and organization development, and an MBA in management and an MA in organizational psychology from Fairleigh Dickinson University. He earned his undergraduate degree from Rutgers College.

Bill is a resident of Westfield, New Jersey. He may be contacted at wmskane@aol.com.

Acknowledgments

I would like to thank several people for their faith in me during this project, including

Coach John Wooden and Andy Hill for their confidence and enthusiasm.

Jennifer Simon of Pearson for this opportunity.

Russ Hall and John D. Kammeyer-Mueller for their editorial eyes.

Rob Gilbert and Richard White for their faith and prodding, and sounding-board guidance.

My professional colleagues Andy O'Connor (Jr. and Sr.), Carolyn Ott, Frank Palma, Kathy Strickland, Dale Winston, Laurie Murphy, Marcia Glatman, Emil Vogel, Bob Mintz, Keith Mullin, Phil Masin, Mike Brenner, Susan Bishop, Stuart Lipper, and Bob Marino.

My academic advisors of influence through the years: Bob Chell, Paul Strauss, Keith Melville, and Charlie Seashore.

Some present and former coworkers, especially Bill Cassidy, Jerry Senion, John Warren, David Owen, Tom Moran, Raj Sinha, Dick Furlaud, Paul Maccaro, Shigeru Kobayashi, Phil Chaikin, and Phyllis Lockwood.

Friends Jim Johnson, Terri Freeman, Bob Cahill, Laura and Rodger Studwell, Bob Lackaye, Tom Decker, Rick Elliott, Bret Schundler, Neil Horne, the late Gary Kehler, Holly Robertson, Franci Ferguson, George Clay, and the late Pat Hyland.

Brothers Dennis and Bob; and especially David for his ongoing support.

Sons Billy, David, and Michael for their tolerance and patience.

My wife Coleen for her love and endless encouragement that withstood many of my tests.

My late mother for her heart; my father for his lap.

You're all very special.